Agre

Agree to Win by Willbourn, Hugh

Other books by Hugh Willbourn:
How to Mend Your Broken Heart (with Paul McKenna)

Agree to Win

ESSENTIAL STEPS TO NEGOTIATE IN YOUR WORK AND LIFE

HUGH WILLBOURN

BBC
BOOKS

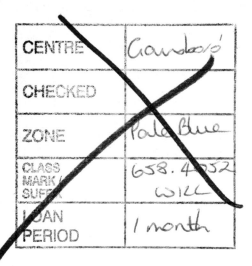

Published by BBC Books, BBC Worldwide Limited,
Woodlands, 80 Wood Lane, London W12 0TT

First published 2004.
Copyright © Hugh Willbourn 2004
The moral right of the author has been asserted.

ISBN 0 563 52148 1

Commissioning Editor: Emma Shackleton
Project Editor: Mari Roberts
Designer: Ann Thompson
Production Controller: Christopher Tinker

Set in Frutiger
Printed and bound in Great Britain by Mackays of Chatham

I would like to thank all the excellent negotiators –
friends, clients, colleagues and students –
whose work has inspired and informed this book

Contents

Agree to Win

You already have all the skills you need

Chapter 1
You can negotiate

❑ Activate your talents

❑ How this book works

❑ The necessity of practice

❑ What metaphors do you use?

You don't have to be powerful to negotiate. You don't have to be rich. You don't have to be a genius. Everyone can negotiate. You don't need any more than you have right now. This book will show you how to use what you have to get more of what you want.

When you negotiate you get what you want by reaching agreement. That's why negotiation is such an excellent skill – not only do you get what you want, but you get it with the agreement and cooperation of other people. Negotiation creates positive relationships.

It also creates wealth. If you want, you can use it to become rich and powerful. But negotiation is not necessarily about money and power. It can help you get on better with your family, settle arguments with your partner and build friendships in your neighbourhood. Negotiation skills will help you in every area of your life, and in this book we will explore examples from all sorts of different contexts.

Negotiation is good for you too. The more you negotiate, the more experience you gain, the more you increase your personal responsibility and power, and the more satisfaction you feel. The more you negotiate for yourself, the more you run your life on your own terms.

Sounds pretty wonderful, doesn't it? Well, it is. Learning to negotiate is like learning to swim. There's no downside. You don't have to swim if you don't want to, but if you find yourself in three metres of water you will be glad of the ability. And you'll find that negotiating, like swimming, is enjoyable. You don't have to be a full-time business executive to enjoy it, any more than you need to be an Olympic athlete to enjoy swimming.

Whether you are building a business or trying to lead a quiet life, negotiation will help you get more of what you want, with the cooperation of other people.

■ Make this book pay for itself

This book could be the biggest bargain of your life. If you use just one tenth of the techniques in this book on just one tenth of the occasions when you buy, sell or trade something, you will save more than its cover price before a week has passed. The means to save huge amounts of money lies in your hands.

But more important than money, you can use negotiation to create solutions in other areas of your life. It can help you reduce stress, have more positive and productive relationships, get more respect, and assert your own values in your life. You don't have to choose from alternatives created by other people – you can create the type of opportunities, jobs and relationships that you want to enjoy in your life.

Matthew had a sales job in the marine industry. He liked his job, he liked his customers and he liked his salary, but he didn't like his boss. It was time to move on. Unfortunately, no jobs were advertised that he thought would suit him. After actively looking for months, Matthew asked himself where he wanted to work and what seemed to him to be the best next step in his career. He decided that he should really go to work for one of his current firm's competitors. They had management he respected and a product he felt he could sell. They did not, however, have a position equivalent to his own into which he could move. So he went to see the man he wanted to work for and persuaded him to create the job and then employ him to fill it. If, like Matthew, you can't see the opportunity you want to take up, like him you can use your negotiation skills to create it.

■ Emotional resources

This book will teach you to negotiate. Even more importantly, this book will show you how to summon the emotional and psychological resources you need to negotiate effectively and powerfully. In other words, you'll find out not just what to do, but how to prepare yourself to do it.

In the various strands of my career I work in the fields of negotiation, business, research, psychotherapy, education, writing and performance arts. In all of these, not just the first, negotiation is a vital skill.

Because it has for so long been an interest of mine, I talk to the people I meet in all these different fields about negotiation. I like to collect stories of successful deals. But when people tell me about negotiations in which they didn't get what they wanted, I ask them what went wrong. Over and over again I hear the reply, 'I knew what I should have done, but I just couldn't do it.' They knew the theory of negotiation, but they didn't know how to access the inner resources that would allow them to use their intellectual knowledge. Here, you are going to find out not just what to do, not just why to do it, but the specific psychological techniques that allow you to do exactly what you need to do, whatever the circumstances and no matter with whom you are negotiating.

■ How this book works

Chapter 2 outlines the core characteristics of a good negotiator and gives you strategies, exercises and techniques to help develop each one. Some of the techniques have evolved from my work in psychotherapy and hypnosis, some of them from my work with Paul McKenna and other modern, practical self-development experts. All of them have been tested thoroughly by me and by others, and proven over and over again to work. Some are short and simple; others are longer. Work carefully through them, applying one hundred per cent of your commitment and concentration.

Because these techniques create new relationships with certain parts of your mind and mental capabilities, some of them can seem strange, even silly, at first. That's no excuse not to use them. Building up the power of your mind and creating emotional strength is just like going to the gym. If you are rather unfit you might feel a bit embarrassed getting on a running machine, going red in the face and having to get off after half a mile. But each time you do it, you get a bit fitter and you feel a bit better. Then, when the results begin to show, you don't feel silly at all. In fact, you feel fit, healthy and proud of yourself. It's just the same with your mental and emotional powers. Even if you feel self-conscious doing these exercises at first, you will very soon feel confident, relaxed and capable.

Chapters 3 to 7 take you through the overall process of negotiation. Chapter 3 outlines what you need to do before you open negotiations with the other party. The better your preparation, the better you will negotiate. Your preparation will include gathering information and assessing it, deciding on your goals and establishing your style of negotiation. You might have to make a choice about the time and place to negotiate, and you must always think about what could go wrong, as well as what you want to go right.

Chapter 4 is about opening: the first moves of negotiation. You will learn how to get the attention of the other party, how to establish rapport and how to judge the best opening offer.

Chapter 5 discusses a range of the major strategies and techniques in negotiation. You will explore different ways of supporting your proposal and bringing the other party into agreement with your offers. You will learn how to vary your offer while preserving its value to you, and how to address gambits aimed at reducing your power.

Chapter 6 examines the difficulties that can arise and how to deal with them. It looks at complex negotiations in different parts of life: social and domestic, as well as business. You will learn how to negotiate with unwilling partners, and how to re-start negotiations that have ground to a halt.

Chapter 7 looks at closing a deal. You will learn how to bring negotiations to a satisfactory conclusion and how to ensure that you get what you want. The chapter also outlines the essential points you should check before signing any contract.

Finally, Chapter 8 reviews the whole process and shows you how to use each and every negotiation to enhance your own skills and the core characteristics of a competent, confident negotiator.

■ The value of practice

With all of the techniques there is one straightforward way to learn them and reap their benefits. Practice. The more you practise the better you get. When you have done enough practice you will have taught your unconscious mind the process and you will be able to use the techniques fluently with almost no effort at all.

It is that easy. But you do have to practise. Over and over again. And the ones you need to practise are the ones that don't come easily to you. Many of these exercises will be easy, because you already have the skills you need and all you are learning is how to transfer them to the arena of negotiations. But some of them will appear more challenging at first. Practise those.

You may feel by now that I am perhaps over-emphasizing the issue of practice. I'm doing so because remarkably often a client agrees with me that they are going to practise something and when next we meet, they haven't. On enquiry I discover that they tried the exercise once, they understood how it worked and what it was meant to do for them, and so they didn't do any more practice. It is a very easy, very common error to confuse comprehension with competence. Because we grasp something intellectually we tend to believe we can also carry out the behaviour just as easily. This is not true. In order to integrate the learning into your behavioural repertoire, you need to practise it. Functional memory is created by repetition.

It is rather like learning the lines of a play or learning a poem by heart. You have to read the text over and over again. Then you have to repeat the words over and over, at first with the text, then without. The repetition creates a pattern of neural pathways in your brain so that one day you only need to say the first line for all the others to follow automatically.

Learning anything by heart is not at all difficult; it only requires repetition. It is the same with the psychological and strategic techniques in this book. Practise them over and over and over again, then, when you need them, they will be there automatically, ready for you to use.

■ Learning from stories

You will learn tactics and techniques covering all the different stages of negotiation. There are stories throughout the book from all sorts of situations to illustrate how these tactics can be used. On first reading you might think all this represents a formidable challenge to your memory. Don't worry. You don't have to remember every single technique at every twist and turn of negotiation. As you read the book and practise the exercises, you are letting the learning soak into your memory and your unconscious mind.

As you practise each technique or tip, you build it into your repertoire so that in time it comes naturally to you in just the same way as you integrate other complex skills, like dancing or driving a car. After a while you even forget how much you've learned.

I entered the field of psychotherapy through the study of hypnosis. Several years after my first training I needed to get another certificate to validate my membership of a society of therapists. I had to pass written and practical exams to demonstrate my competence. In the practical we had to conduct a short interview with a patient while being observed by the examiner. A young man was shown in and I started chatting to him to make him feel comfortable. He told me a bit about himself and I thought we were getting on fine when suddenly I noticed that more than ten of our allotted twenty minutes had passed. I thought I'd better get down to work. He was interested in hypnosis so I showed him a simple arm levitation, in which the subject's arm feels weightless and rises without conscious effort. When the interview had ended I turned to the examiner and shrugged. I was a bit embarrassed at having spent so much time just chatting.

To my astonishment she shook her head and laughed. Then she showed me her notes. According to her, I had started to hypnotize my subject within forty seconds of him walking into the room. She had several pages of notes of all the hypnotic language patterns, gestures and techniques I had used in my 'chat'.

The point of the story is not to boast – much – but to show how patterns of thought, behaviour and language, which I had made such a conscious effort to learn just a few years earlier, had become so habitual that I didn't even notice I was using them.

You will find the same thing happens to you as you practise your negotiation skills. As you practise, you will make everything you learn from this book your own. You will build your own style from your own unique resources and the universal skills of negotiation and confidence that you are learning right now.

All the stories in the book are true, but I have changed all the names and some of the identifying details in order to preserve the privacy of those involved. Each one of them illustrates one or more significant elements of negotiation. I have gathered them from colleagues, clients and successful negotiators in all walks of life.

Stories are a great way to learn. They are much easier to follow and far more fun than dry, theoretical explanations. But these stories can be far more than examples for you, if you want. An excellent way for you to learn even more from these stories is to imagine vividly taking part in them yourself. With each story, you can imagine being the person conducting the negotiation.

First of all, read them through several times and build up a clear picture of what happens. Fill in the details so that you have turned each story into a short film in your mind. Visualize the people, hear the sound of their voices and create a feeling of the surroundings of the situation, the weather, the lighting and the temperature.

Next, imagine stepping into the shoes of the successful negotiator. Imagine what you can see through these eyes, what you can hear with these ears and what you feel in this position. Feel the actual feelings you have in relationship with the other people in the stories: not knowing what will happen, making the moves and saying the words, feeling the tension, the humour and all the other elements of the occasion.

It is not only fun to imagine yourself in other people's situations, it is also a profound and intense learning experience. Medical researchers and sports psychologists have discovered that the mind and body respond to vividly imagined experiences in the same way as they do to real events. Leading athletes and sportsmen and women use this principle to improve their game by mental rehearsal. The power of mental rehearsal has been demonstrated over and over again. A good example is an experiment in which two basketball teams were compared. The first team spent an hour practising physically, and then had their performance tested. The second team spent the hour visualizing scoring successfully over and over again. Then they were tested. The team that had visualized, but not physically practised, achieved a far greater improvement from their base level of performance.

Of course, it is vital that they had the experience of playing basketball in the first place. Visualization cannot substitute completely for practising the basic motor skills. However, when you have the skills, visualization is one of the fastest ways to improve them.

The same principle holds true with negotiation. As well as vividly imagining yourself in the stories, you must also practise the techniques and read the book thoroughly. But, like the basketball players, you have all the basic skills already. You have all you need to start negotiating – what you are learning now is how to deploy your skills and how to link them up so as to be most effective.

When you vividly recreate a negotiation scenario in your mind, you are rehearsing all the skills and emotional resourcefulness that person used in that situation. You are teaching your unconscious mind to emulate within yourself the responses of a first-class negotiator. By sharing their histories you are echoing their feelings and sensations and you are teaching yourself to achieve success in the same sort of way.

■ Optimizing your metaphors

I have talked about techniques and strategies but, as we shall see in the next chapter, the roots of success in negotiation lie not only in techniques but also in attitude, in your way of being. Before we look at your attributes as a negotiator, take a moment to ask yourself how you think of negotiation. What words do you use to describe it? What do you naturally compare it to?

Most of us unconsciously structure our understanding of negotiation by reference to an underlying metaphor. For example, a very common metaphor for negotiation is a battle. This metaphor lies beneath phrases such as 'winning position', 'crushing the opposition' and 'gaining ground'. These vivid and powerful metaphors have a great influence on our understanding of negotiation, and hence on our actions. If you see negotiation as a battle, it will have a tendency to turn into one. You will find you feel as though you are in combat. Anything you trade with the other party will feel like a loss or a concession and your attitude will tend to be one of trying to conquer them. Naturally enough they will pick that up and fight back.

If you do have a tendency to compare negotiation to fighting it can be instructive to ask yourself whether you are behaving as a foot soldier or a general. A soldier asks few questions. Effectively he has to fight whatever is in front of him. A general, however, has to maintain an overview of the entire situation. He must be aware of the whole battle, indeed the conduct of the whole war. He will know that to win he has to deploy his forces tactically, fighting just to hold some positions, feinting in other places and attacking fiercely at selected weak spots. In all but the simplest negotiations it is better to think like a general than a foot soldier.

Another common group of metaphors for negotiation is games. For some it is like a card game such as bridge or poker. This gives rise to metaphors such as 'winning hand' and 'trumping your offer'. Many other games have lent analogies to negotiation, including snooker, tennis and chess.

If you naturally compare negotiation to a game then the various moves and manoeuvres of the game will suggest analogous possibilities in negotiation. You might think of a strategy that 'snookers' your opponent, preventing him from aiming directly at his goal. You might attempt to 'serve an ace' to which he is unable to respond, or you might seek to limit his options until he is in 'checkmate'. Each game suggests different possibilities, and in fact much of the time we tend to use a mixture of many different metaphors.

Negotiation tends to flow more easily when thought of as a game than when thought of as a battle, but it remains a competitive activity.

Construction is another common metaphor for negotiation, which has the advantage of a less oppositional flavour. Talk of 'solid foundations' and 'building relationships' draws on the construction metaphor and tends to produce a more cooperative feeling in the process.

It can be helpful and enlightening to begin deliberately to use metaphors from other human activities to describe negotiation. These other metaphors help you to think of new and creative possibilities in negotiation by analogy with their own internal procedures.

You could, for example, compare negotiation to dancing, where two people move together round a room. One leads and the other follows, ornamenting the steps. The fundamental analogy is one of cooperation rather than competition.

Alternatively, you could compare negotiation to gardening. You can think of planting seeds, weeding beds, supporting seedlings, training climbers, pruning bushes and so forth. This will give rise to all sorts of notions around growing and nurturing possibilities.

Negotiation can also be compared to romance. One party is the suitor to the other. There are stages of flirtation, of double messages, of seduction and so on. The metaphor of romance implies attraction but also includes the possibility of playing hard to get. Romance asks for proof of affections and challenges a suitor to earn his reward with a compelling demonstration of his love. And love affairs, like negotiations, have their ups and downs.

One of my own favourite metaphors is fishing. Imagine you are standing on the riverbank. You cast a fly and a salmon goes for it. Your task now is to land the fish. In other words, you want to reel the fish in to yourself, you do not intend to go out into the river. You have to keep firm pressure on, but not so strong that it breaks the line, nor haul so hard that you pull the hook out of the fish's mouth. If it is a large and strong fish you must take your time. You may have to let the fish swim up and down the river until it tires. Whenever it pulls less strongly you reel it in; when it pulls you let out some line, only to haul it back in again as it tires again. The ultimate aim of fishing is to land the fish. This metaphor clarifies the distinction between negotiation and compromise. In a compromise, maybe you would get only half of the fish, or half of the time the fish would pull you into the river. When you land a deal you get the whole fish where you want it, on the riverbank.

■ YOUR METAPHORS

- ■ Imagine you are telling a friend about a deal that you are working on.
- ■ Listen to your own use of language and make a note of the metaphors that lie beneath the words you use.
- ■ Make up some new metaphors that compare negotiation to something you are good at and enjoy.

A conversation leading to an agreement

Chapter 2
Being a negotiator

❑ Negotiation is enjoyable

❑ The characteristics of a good negotiator

❑ Techniques to enhance your skills and attributes

A negotiation is a conversation leading to an agreement. The conversation doesn't have to be loud, it doesn't have to be long, it doesn't have to be astonishing. If you are new to negotiating, don't be put off by stories of other people's amazing deals. Remember, the deals people boast about are the ones they are most proud of. The everyday deals, and the ones that didn't work out, don't receive the same publicity, even though they are far more common. For every staggeringly lucrative deal, there are dozens of just reasonable ones that make a decent sum of money or settle an ordinary dispute.

Whether you are negotiating for business or in social and family situations, your deals do not need to be spectacular to be satisfactory. Sometimes part of the success of family negotiations is that they are low-key. Disagreements may be loud and dramatic; reconciliation is often easier when it is quiet and gentle.

The different elements of negotiation that you will learn about here make up that conversation. There are textbooks and treatises which have analysed the subject in great detail and given names to all the various stages, tactics, styles and activities that make up a negotiation. This analysis gives the impression that negotiation is a lot more complicated, and a lot more boring, than it is in real life. Negotiation is not complicated. Negotiators do not have to memorize long lists of techniques or carry out long and tedious analyses of tactics and positions.

Negotiation is fun. Almost every time I negotiate something I enjoy the process. All the negotiators I know enjoy what they do. When I interviewed the remarkable people who contributed their insights and stories to this book, I wasn't bored once.

I realized as I listened to their stories that they do not see negotiation as a science. Nor do they see it as an art. Negotiation is just part of their way of life. It comes naturally to them. They have learned how to do it in the same way as you and I learned how to walk and talk.

And when you know how to walk and talk, you don't keep thinking about it. For 99 per cent of the time you forget all about it. It's like learning how to play a game. When you know what to do, you don't keep thinking about it. You just do what you need to when you judge it to be necessary. In the same way, as you integrate the attitudes and skills of negotiation, you naturally get better and better all the time with less and less conscious effort. If you can communicate with your fellow humans, you already have all the skills you need.

You begin negotiating by starting a conversation. In fact, negotiation is easier than making conversation because you already have something you want to talk about. Even if you don't mention it immediately, you know where you are heading. I have found that even people who were convinced they were too shy to make conversation or to approach strangers found it easier to do so when they were negotiating.

■ Any time, any place

Negotiations can take place anywhere, any time, with anyone about anything. That's a pretty broad range of circumstances to deal with! But good negotiators really can do that. The tendency to think about negotiation in terms of money obscures the reality that negotiations cover every area of life from romance to politics and nursery to boardroom. It is not just traders who negotiate. Every job and every family calls for negotiation.

It would be baffling trying to conjure up a list of essential techniques in every situation that called for negotiation. Luckily, it's not necessary. Every negotiation is unique, so becoming an excellent negotiator is not a matter of stringing together an ever more sophisticated pattern of techniques, like a concert violinist. Of course, you will be able to use all the techniques you come across, but the very essence of success in negotiation is not technical mastery. Good negotiators do deals the way a good yachtsman sails his boat. The yachtsman doesn't fill his mind with techniques or rituals, he concentrates on where he is going and responds to all the changes in the weather. And yachtsmen enjoy their sailing. Similarly, the negotiator is not juggling concepts and techniques in his mind, he is focused on what he's trying to achieve.

In fact, for a successful negotiator, the arrangements they negotiate and the deals they do are not separate from the rest of their lives. They are simply a part of how they go about being in the world. The deals and arrangements flow from how they see opportunities, how they get on with people and how they apply their creativity to the world.

■ Being a negotiator

The secret of negotiation is a way of being. In other words, you will learn to negotiate successfully, anything, anywhere, by learning to *be a negotiator*. Your way of being is the sum total of your attitudes, habits of mind, modes of interpretation and emotional disposition. Much of it is based on your character, which you have acquired through your genes and your environment. A lot of it is formed by attitudes and habits acquired unintentionally as you passed through life and education.

As you learn to be a negotiator you will not only remain true to yourself, you will actually become more true to yourself, because by negotiation you will be asserting your own values and creating deals that realize them in the world. When you negotiate successfully with your in-laws over how long they come to stay with you, you will be getting their agreement to an arrangement that suits you, instead of putting up with whatever they want – which ultimately will be better for you all.

Being a negotiator entails developing certain aspects of your character. We all have these abilities to some extent, but some are more developed than others. To realize your potential as a negotiator you will develop these aspects so that they become a larger, but no less natural, part of your way of being.

A way of being includes a way of life, a way of seeing things, a style of interaction and many other elements. It is part of what makes up being you. You are unique. So as you read the ideas below and practise the suggestions, think of it as broadening your range and including and activating more of your abilities. You are not getting rid of anything at all. You are simply adding more possibilities and activating your talents.

You will use certain techniques and develop your strategic repertoire as well, but remember the foundation of negotiation is not technique but attitude. If you find yourself in a tense situation and you don't know what to do and you can't think of a single 'technique', don't worry. Simply use what comes naturally to you. That's what Tom Hart Dyke did when he and his friend were captured by guerrillas in Central America.[1] They had no idea what their captors intended. They were in fear for their lives, being marched through the jungle to an unknown destination, when Tom spotted a rare and beautiful orchid. With a cry of joy he rushed over to it and began to examine it while talking nineteen to the dozen. His captors were completely perplexed but curious.

Eventually Tom's enthusiasm for orchids and rare plants created a bridge of empathy with the guerrillas. Initially he had nothing to negotiate with, but by creating sympathy and interest he won concessions and friendship from them. The relationship that built up contributed to their safety and to their eventual release.

■ Virtuous circle

You will find that negotiating gets easier and easier. As you develop the attitudes and attributes of a negotiator, it will come naturally to you. Furthermore, all the attributes of a negotiator are natural parts of the human character and hence extremely easy to develop. Most of the time all you need to do is to remember to activate that part of your character. It really is that simple.

For the sake of simplicity I have isolated the central qualities of a negotiator and discussed each one separately. The art of negotiation involves being:

optimistic

a good listener   curious

powerful   aware

authentic   solution-
                                              focused

persuasive   thrifty

flexible   goal-
                                              orientated

at ease
with money   tough

relaxed   persistent

sociable   realistic

confident

These characteristics are not a standard you have to attain; they are more like directions or attitudes. You can do a little more of them and get a little more used to them every day. You are not seeking to pass an exam, but rather to increase your range of possibilities. In many ways a lot of them overlap. Persistency and confidence, for example, have a lot in common. More importantly, however, not only do they overlap but each of these qualities contributes to some or all of the others. So as you practise one, it assists you with others at the same time.

As we grew up each of us will have developed each characteristic to a different degree, so each one of us will have to concentrate more on some elements than others. It doesn't matter at what level you start, because every improvement will contribute to your success. Nor does it matter how you rate yourself or others at this moment. There is no need to be perfect in every respect. You will find, however, that the more you negotiate, the more these qualities are brought to the fore and the more you identify with them.

GETTING STARTED

- Choose an issue or a challenge in your own life right now that you would like to resolve by negotiation. Write it down.
- As you go through this book, note down ideas and techniques that will be helpful.
- Use the suggestions and exercises throughout the book to practise them.
- When the opportunity arises, use the ideas and techniques in your own real-life situation.

Optimistic

A successful negotiator is optimistic. Optimists believe that things will turn out well. Most of us are optimistic sometimes. What is startling about good negotiators is that they are optimistic almost all of the time.

Optimism in itself tends to work like a virtuous circle. Optimistic people bring a positive outlook to any situation, which tends to have a positive effect, which in turn increases the chances of a positive outcome. This reinforces the optimism with which they started out, and so it goes on.

Whatever the situation, optimists are always focused on the rewarding aspects of it. If the sun is shining, you enjoy it. If it is raining, you appreciate that gardens and crops need the rain, and you remember that sooner or later the sun will come out again. You are not blind to difficulties or problems, but your energies and attention are always focused on whatever there is to enjoy or to work towards.

Of course, sometimes things work out for the best and sometimes they don't. So what does an optimistic negotiator do if things don't turn out well? *You move the goal posts, so that whatever happens is seen as an ongoing movement towards success.*

Brendan buys and sells classic sports cars. It is not his main business but he likes the cars, he likes driving them and he likes negotiating enough good deals to make his hobby pay for itself. He had been trying to buy an old Alfa Romeo for weeks when he found one day that it had been sold to someone else. He was annoyed to miss the bargain, but he soon moved the goal posts. He reframed the time and effort he had put into the negotiations as part of building up a good relationship with the car dealer so that he would be well placed to get the next bargain when it came along. In other words his 'failure' was seen as a stage on the route to a future success.

Because optimism increases the chances of success it also increases the credibility of your negotiation proposals. In negotiating family disputes there is often no financial incentive. It may be that your belief that an acceptable resolution is possible is the only factor you have available with which to get a dialogue going. Don't underestimate the power of it. A survey was conducted among successful psychotherapists. The therapists were asked how they thought they had helped their clients. They gave a lot of interesting and often very different answers.

The clients were then asked what they thought the therapists had done that had helped them. The clients hardly mentioned any of the complicated interventions mentioned by the therapists. They said it was the positive attitude of the therapist that made the difference. They believed that their therapist believed in them, and that made it easier for them to believe in themselves.

Optimism is therapeutic. You don't even need to know exactly what you want to be optimistic. In fact, sometimes it is positively helpful to be vague. When I am travelling I tend to think I'll find a nice place to stay and a nice place to eat, although I don't know what precisely I will find. As a result, if I see hotels or restaurants that don't seem very attractive, I keep going until I find one that really does appeal to me. This can take some time and occasionally tries the patience of my partner.

On one occasion the Californian hotel I had been recommended turned out to be a pastiche of an English Victorian guesthouse; not to my taste. We drove 25 miles to another hotel recommended for its local colour. The room they had kept for us overlooked the kitchen air-conditioning unit. We turned back, and stopped to look at a place calling itself a motel. It turned out to have a delightful little apartment with its own deck giving directly onto a beautiful lake, and it was half the price of the recommended hotels.

If I didn't believe I'd find a nice place I would have accepted the first one I saw and I'd never have found anything better. My experience has taught me that, generally, if I keep going I do find what I want. So my optimism reinforces itself.

Optimism is infectious too. On the whole it is more fun to smile and to enjoy life. The more you smile the more you remind the people you meet that they can do so too. And as making someone else smile makes you feel good, the virtuous circle kicks off again.

Even in difficult situations it is worth remembering that in the end things will get better. Optimism does not entail being unrealistic about the difficulties in life. Albert Reynolds was one of the principal architects of the peace process in Northern Ireland, which has brought about a great reduction in sectarian violence. When he was asked what he thought would happen in the future, he replied, 'There will be peace.' He knows as well as any man the long, deep historical roots of the conflict and all the problems that have been exacerbated by the conflict and the violence over centuries. Yet he believes that eventually there will be peace.

And whatever troubles there are before that peace is established, his belief in that ultimate resolution has had a powerful effect on what has been achieved so far.

Reframing

Optimism is a habit of seeing that, whatever the situation, there are positive possibilities. The simplest way to do this is to reframe your situation in terms of a positive outcome. When we talk or think about our experience there is always an implicit frame around it – just as a picture is mounted with a frame around it. In fact, there are many frames around our experience, and one of them is always the emotional frame. If I say, 'I had a rotten day, my car wouldn't start and I had to walk into town', my frame is one of criticism and negativity. I feel let down and inconvenienced by the car's breakdown. If I say, 'My car wouldn't start today, so I had to walk into town, which meant I got some exercise', I have reframed the same event in terms of a positive outcome. I may have experienced annoyance and frustration for a time, but I also found a more positive way to frame what happened.

It may sound a little simplistic spelt out like this, but occasionally a little dose of simplicity can work wonders in transforming our lives. Looking on the bright side is often simple.

Being negative, on the other hand, is often complicated and, strangely, that can make it seem more real or more important. After all, if I am thinking about my feelings and the disruption to my plans and all the rearrangements I had to make to deal with not having enough time to stick to my original plan because I had to walk into town instead of driving, it is quite enough to fill my head with all sorts of bother, let alone make a heck of a long sentence to write out. But it doesn't make resenting all that more important. It might just be that you really needed to get that exercise.

Reframing means putting a different frame of reference around your experience. Which frame you choose is up to you. You can change your mood, and learn more from your experience, when you choose an optimistic as opposed to a negative frame. The facts remain the same, but by changing your frame you change your own reaction, and can turn even apparently unfavourable situations to your advantage.

I add, however, a word of caution: don't fake your optimism. Find a real basis for it. If you use positive words but don't find or feel a genuine benefit in your situation, then that's not optimism, it's bullshit. Human beings are remarkably sensitive to bullshit. You won't fool anyone else, and you won't fool yourself. Many people will be too polite to tell you that you are bullshit-ting, but they won't be fooled.

In every situation, find your own inner reason for optimism. This does not mean pretending that bad things have not happened. Rather, it is a matter of accepting the difficulties and losses of life, but at the same time affirming the constant creation of possibilities of things getting better again. The more often you activate your optimism, the more naturally it will spring to mind so that it becomes a part of your everyday response to the world. When that happens you have laid a firm foundation for negotiating success.

ENHANCING YOUR OPTIMISM

- Whatever you are negotiating, frame your desired outcome in positive terms.
- If you feel as if something has gone wrong, think of three ways, how ever small, in which the situation is a benefit.
- Every day ask yourself: What can I do today to make my life more rewarding?

Curious

A good negotiator is naturally interested in life. He or she has a healthy curios-ity about the unknown, and a sense that whatever it reveals will be worth exploring.

Ernest Rossi tells a story about a time when he was training with Dr Milton H. Erickson, the renowned and extraordinary American psychiatrist whose papers he later edited. Erickson was interviewing a couple who were having relationship difficulties, and after ten minutes or so he asked the hus-band to leave the room. When he was gone, Erickson leaned forward and asked the woman, 'How long have you been cheating on your husband?'

At the end of the session Rossi asked Erickson how on earth he knew that the woman was cheating on her husband. 'Well,' replied Erickson, 'I've never met a woman who sat like that who wasn't cheating, but I'll be very curious to find one who isn't.'

Erickson's skill at reading non-verbal behaviour was astonishing. You might think that if he could read people like a book he would just sit back and do so. He, however, thought the opposite. He was very curious to find an exception to the knowledge he had already accumulated. Erickson ascribed much of his own learning to being insatiably curious. Even if you reach that level of insight you can still, like Erickson, be curious.

Being curious means that you learn more, which in turn increases your knowledge, and that is likely to be helpful. But it's not just that more knowledge is a good thing. Because negotiation is such a dynamic process, you can never be sure that you know what knowledge will be useful or when. In fact, over and over again I heard stories that people got amazing deals because they just happened to have found out the right piece of information out of pure curiosity.

Brendan, who buys and sells sports cars, went to an auction because he had an eye on a Ferrari that was entered in it, although he suspected that it would go for more than he could afford. It did. But as he was there, he had a snoop around the other lots and saw an old Mercedes SL. There was an unpleasant smell in the car and, being curious, Brendan investigated. He poked about a bit and saw that it had a brand-new soft-top fitted. Putting two and two together he realized that the previous owner must have stored it with the hood wet. The fabric had rotted and caused the nasty smell. They had replaced the hood, but the smell still lingered.

When the car came up in the auction no one was bidding for it, so just as the auctioneer was about to call the car in Brendan made a bid and got the car for less than half of its book value. Before the end of the auction he had been offered a price that would have made him a handsome profit by other buyers who realized what they had missed. Brendan kept the car. The smell was gone in a couple of weeks. If he hadn't investigated a bit further and worked out what the smell was, he wouldn't have bid, and he wouldn't have the car he is driving around town to this day.

Curiosity gives you a significant advantage when you come to negotiate. As you are naturally curious, you are habitually gathering information all the time, so you will be one step ahead of any other party who only starts gathering information when they decide they are going to negotiate a deal.

Curiosity is also an excellent habit to have in situations where you do not know whether the other party is trustworthy. People can take offence if you appear to question their integrity, but innocent, healthy curiosity will often get you all the information you need without any offence at all.

And curiosity doesn't just help you when you know you are going to be negotiating – it is often the starting point of creating a deal that you didn't even know was going to happen.

Duncan has an aircraft-leasing business. While negotiating a deal he found himself waiting around at an airport in the Balkans. He went for a little stroll, had a look inside a hangar and saw a long line of jet fighters being worked on. Being curious, he asked what was going on and discovered that they were being upgraded. He didn't know at the time, any more than you do now, how that information was going to be useful. He was just curious.

Good negotiators gather information all the time because they enjoy it. If you are always gently curious and questioning, the world becomes a treasure chest of interests and possibilities. Your curiosity will lead you to see and to create opportunities for negotiation and deals that you would never have even thought of had you not asked that one, curious, question.

Finally, curiosity increases your engagement with people and that, as we will see, is also a significant benefit to a negotiator. If you are genuinely interested in something, your interest will tend to spark a genuine desire to inform in the other person. Furthermore, if you are interested, other people will find you interesting.

The easiest way to increase our curiosity is to remind ourselves how much we don't know and that it is all right not to know. The competitive, information-orientated world around us can create the impression that successful people know huge amounts of information. This is far from the case. Successful people know how to find out what they need to know. And they all start by not knowing. The most original and successful people never take anything for granted and are continually on the alert for new information. They are always curious.

There is absolutely nothing to be ashamed of in not knowing. On the contrary, it is the basis of all learning. However much you happen to know, more important still is your awareness of how much you don't know. That is the doorway to creativity and invention. And in asking questions about what you don't know, you foster your sense of curiosity.

In every situation there are thousands of potential questions to be asked. How do things work? What are they made of and what do they cost? Where do they come from and where are they going? Who are the people involved? What are they like and what do they like? What are their ambitions and dreams? What are their fears? What talents, hobbies and interests do they have? Everyone is fascinating when you find out what interests them, so use your questions to get them talking about their passions.

Soon you will find that your renewed curiosity about the world becomes self-sustaining, because the habit of asking questions breeds more questions.

■ INCREASING YOUR CURIOSITY

- ■ Practise letting people know that you don't know.
- ■ Ask more questions.
- ■ Remember Kipling's famous verse:

   I keep six honest serving men
   They taught me all I knew
   Their names are What and Why and When
   And How and Where and Who.

■ Aware

Great negotiators have a broad and clear awareness of their situation. This doesn't mean they are tense; on the contrary, their normal state is quite relaxed. But along with their curiosity about what is behind the current situation, they are alert to what is actually present. They enjoy noticing things.

Professor Richard Wiseman of the University of Hertfordshire has published some fascinating work on luck.[2] His research has shown that luck is not arbitrary. It is not mysterious or fated. It is a function of how we see the world. Lucky people are more alert and open to chance opportunities than unlucky ones. When he taught 'unlucky' people to become more alert and to notice opportunities, their luck improved.

One of his elegant experiments demonstrates just how differently lucky and unlucky people saw the world. You might think you would notice a £5 note lying on the pavement in front of you, wouldn't you? Well, Professor Wiseman's experiments demonstrated that unlucky people are far less likely to notice random good fortune. An unlucky person will walk straight past money on the ground, while the lucky person behind notices it.

If a psychologist asked you to look through a newspaper and count the photographs in it you might expect you'd notice a half-page advertisement in type more than one and half inches high telling you how many photographs there were. You might think you would also notice another half-page advert reading, 'Stop counting. Tell the experimenter you have seen this and win £100.' In Wiseman's experiments, none of his unlucky participants noticed either advertisement.

Why didn't the unlucky people see the money or the helpful advert? It seems that the field of their attention is too narrow. If they are asked to count photographs, that is all they do. Keen to get it right, but knowing that they've made silly mistakes in the past, they are nervous lest they get it wrong, so they tense up and focus completely on the task to the exclusion of all else. They try too hard. They count, and check their counting, and worry about the count going wrong. Effectively they are running three or more separate processes to deliver just one output.

There is a limit to how much we can pay attention to at any one time. Psychologist George Miller conducted a famous experiment in the 1950s that showed we can only hold between five and nine units of information in our short-term memory. Most of us can hold just seven distinct things in our short-term memory. There seems to be a similar limit to our conscious awareness. If counting photographs uses up three of those units, you could be down to as few as two others to process all the rest of the world.

But this excessive effort is truly unnecessary. Our autonomic nervous system, a major component of the unconscious mind, has a marvellous capacity to pick up any divergence from an established norm. This ability to sense change is an integral part of our basic survival system. Once our mind has recognized a pattern it will be hypersensitive to any change in that pattern. Changes in an established pattern could be indicators of potential danger, so our nervous system is set up to alert us to them as soon as possible. The system has been honed by countless generations of evolution and is extremely efficient. When we relax and trust our automatic systems to work for us, there is no need to worry. When we are free of unnecessary worry we have more awareness available to notice more of the world around us.

We use our conscious attention most efficiently when we trust the unconscious mind to help us. And when we do so, it seems completely natural – because it is.

You will not be surprised to hear that good negotiators normally describe themselves as lucky. Their awareness alerts them to opportunities. They are not continuously on the lookout. Rather, they have a sort of relaxed openness, which takes things in all the time. They use all their senses in 360 degrees like a radar system. On a radar screen you can see the beam of radar that continually sweeps round in a circle, illuminating the surrounding objects as it does so. The radar beam keeps circling automatically. As we shall see, this 360-degree vision is very important when you are constructing a deal, because sometimes there are many different factors to keep track of. You need to be aware of changes in the context around you just as much as of the other party's actions and offers.

But rather than needing to switch on your radar each time you negotiate, it is a lot simpler to get used to having it on all the time. If you go on the bridge of a ship you will see that they have the radar on all the time – not just in the fog or the dark – because it is a useful easy way to gather information. You can do the same.

A little while after his trip to the Balkans, Duncan was chatting to a contact who worked for a large European industrial group, whom we shall call ABC. ABC had just agreed to sell a ship to the same country Duncan had recently visited. The ship was to be sold for almost nothing. The profit for ABC would come from the refit it needed. That was going to cost many millions of pounds.

The Balkan country agreed to buy the refit from ABC if ABC would introduce into their economy business equivalent in value to their expenditure on the refit. This is known as an 'offset' deal, and is an increasingly common practice in deals between wealthy countries and less wealthy customers. In order to make the deal go through, ABC needed to find some offset purchasing to be introduced to their client country. Duncan listened intently to his contact's story and went off for lunch with his friend Ivor.

A very simple and effective way to enhance your awareness is simply to remember to notice more about your surroundings. Use all of your senses to become more aware. Ultimately all that we have is our own experience, so the more we appreciate it, the more life we have.

People who survive near-death experiences often talk of the miracle of simply being alive. They have been reminded of the sheer beauty of the natural world and the pleasure we can experience from it.

Meditation, the practice of learning to still the chatter of your mind, also has the effect of letting you be more directly aware of the world around you. No longer distracted by the commentary and worries of the monkey mind, the meditator sees things in their natural, rich simplicity.

However, if meditation seems a bit esoteric there are many other ways to enhance our awareness. For example, my own favourite strategy is to ask an expert. Musicians, sound technicians and recording engineers all have highly developed acoustic sensibility. They can teach you how to listen. Painters and photographers have learned to look at the world in accurate detail. They can teach you how to see. Athletes, dancers and body workers learn to use the balance and perceptions of the body. They can teach you how to feel.

ENRICHING YOUR AWARENESS

- Practise by paying particular attention to just one sensory channel – say, sight – for a whole day. The next day choose another sense, so that after five days you have paid attention to sight, sound, touch, taste and smell. On the sixth day, practise paying attention to your sixth sense, or intuition.
- The following week, concentrate on the sense that you found most difficult to notice.
- Learn by using your senses. Explore activities that use your senses. Learning about photography will enhance your visual discrimination; learning to play a musical instrument will enhance your hearing, and so forth.

> ■ Practise being more exact in your descriptions. As you attempt to describe something accurately, the process of refining your descriptions also refines the understanding you bring to your perceptions.
> ■ Have your radar on all the time.

■ Solution-focused

Social work may seem a million miles from the cut and thrust of market trading, but social workers have to negotiate deals just as important and complex as traders. A social worker helping a family in which a child has been in trouble has to create arrangements with all the different family members as well as meet the requirements of all the different agencies that are involved. Social workers sometimes have to negotiate with five, six or more different parties, each with their own agendas and priorities. Negotiation is a vital part of their skills, although they are of course negotiating not for themselves but for the benefit of others. It's a form of negotiation in which the negotiator is not among the beneficiaries.

Psychotherapists negotiate as well. In fact, psychotherapy is often a process of internal negotiation, helping people to negotiate between all their competing wishes and drives, and helping to integrate them into a coherent, functional, rewarding unity.

In the 1980s, Steve de Shazer and his team of social workers and psychotherapists were operating an unusual family therapy centre in Milwaukee.[3] They had an open appointment system so that people could simply drop in to the centre and if there was a therapist free they could have a session. They had a policy of making their services available to anyone who asked, regardless of income or background.

Many of their clients were people who led very chaotic lives. There were many service users who were part of abusive or poly-abusive families and by any standard of measurement they had a whole heap of troubles. On top of that, many were so disorganized that it was pointless to set up long-term therapy because very few would stay the course. In fact, even showing up for two sessions in a row could not be guaranteed. De Shazer and his colleagues could have tried to get their client group to become more reliable, perhaps by setting up a system of rewards and punishments, or perhaps by laying out fixed contracts. They didn't. Indeed, they recognized that if their clients had been able to order their lives tidily, they wouldn't be in so much need of help.

Rather than get the clients to fit a pre-structured system of therapy, they redesigned their therapy. As the average number of appointments they had with their clients was one, there was little point in spending time on long introductions, taking a history and so forth. Instead, they got straight down to work. They learned to focus immediately on what the clients needed: solutions. And so the phrase was coined: 'solution-focused therapy'.

Solution-focused therapy does what it says. Sometimes the therapists never even ask the client why they've come to therapy. Steve would often open his sessions with the question, 'Are there any times in the recent or distant past in which the problem you are worried about did not occur?' In other words he looks for exceptions to the problem, not at the problem itself.

Over time Steve and his colleagues have built up a repertoire of ideas and questions, all of which guide their clients towards solutions. And they are all very simple questions. In every case they draw their clients' attention to what they are doing successfully, and support them to do more of what works.

Being solution-focused works. The Milwaukee team regularly conduct outcome surveys among their clients and satisfaction rates are very high indeed, even after just one session.

Not surprisingly, news of their work has spread. An enterprising family therapist in Finland called Ben Furman has taken to solution-focused work like a duck to water.[4] He often has to work with families who are polarized or antagonistic, and he has developed a number of approaches that orientate them towards a solution. If, for example, a lot of hostility is expressed at a family meeting and all the parties claim that the situation cannot be resolved, Ben will accept their statements.

'I quite understand,' he will say, 'that it is impossible to move towards a resolution at this meeting. But so that we do not waste our time, I would like to ask each of you the following question. If we were to have a meeting, say, two or three weeks from now, who would have to be present at that meeting in order for us to begin to move towards a solution?' Once again, the focus is on a solution, in an easy and non-threatening way.

Ben also likes to separate problems from people. When he is working with children, for example, he might give the problem behaviour a name. Working with a child who soiled himself regularly he called the problem 'Sneaky Poo' and asked the child what he was doing when he succeeded in stopping 'Sneaky Poo' from creeping into his life. In this way the problem is addressed but blame and shame are avoided. Ben, like Steve and his colleagues, is a great negotiator.

Solution-focused therapy is not complicated. When I first came across it I couldn't believe that something so simple would actually make a real, lasting difference to people's lives. It seemed thoroughly implausible that people with such terrible, profound long-term problems could be genuinely helped by such simple procedures. I kept wanting to offer them clever, complicated solutions to match their twisted and complicated problems.

But of course life isn't like that. Being happy isn't complicated. Being happy may be rich and exciting and vibrant, but it is rarely complicated. It is being in a mess that's complicated. And people in therapy don't need my complicated answers. They already have the solutions they need hidden in their problems. After all, even the awareness that they have a problem is a sign of health, and going to see someone about it means they have already started to address the issue.

Solution-focused therapy is a very practical form of optimism. It not only has faith that all of us can find our own solutions to our problems, it also believes that we are already on the way. Thereafter, it is a process that draws attention to whatever is helpful and progressive and offers encouragement and support to doing more of the same.

Great negotiators are solution-focused. If we apply the model of solution-focused thinking to negotiation we find it fits perfectly. Negotiations may often have a more specific goal than therapy, but the principles are completely compatible. A good negotiator acknowledges obstacles and difficulties but always focuses far more on progress and solutions.

A primary tool of solution-focused work is reframing questions in terms of solutions and resources. For example, rather than asking, 'How come things have got so bad?', a solution-focused negotiator might ask, 'How have we prevented things from getting worse?'

A solution-focused negotiator might begin to broker an agreement between two warring factions by asking someone from each side: 'What would be the smallest indication to you that we will be able to reach an agreement?'

She might ask questions such as: 'Have there been any occasions in the past where you have co-existed peacefully?' A question like this asks about exceptions to the problem. If there is any positive response, the next questions find out the nature of the situation or time in which the problem did not exist. Whenever she finds something that works, the solution-focused negotiator simply asks people to do more of it.

As a general rule, good solutions and good agreements are simple. Complexity is difficult to keep track of and expensive to administer. It also creates more opportunities for mistakes and potentially even for fraud. So the bias towards simplicity in solution-focused thinking is extremely useful and practical.

BECOMING SOLUTION-FOCUSED

- Tackle big problems with small solutions. Ask people to describe what for them would constitute the first, small step towards the solution that is desired.
- Find out what is leading towards the solution you want, and ask for more of it.
- If someone mentions a problem, ask about exceptions, the times when it isn't a problem or the times when it doesn't happen. Ask them what they are doing at that time that is contributing to the absence of the problem, and ask for more of it.
- Separate problems from people and pay close attention to the positive potential of people.
- Pay attention to what people do successfully and encourage more of it.
- Challenge generalized negative comments and look for exceptions.
- Explore generalized positive claims until you arrive at clear, specific, concrete examples of the positive benefits or behaviour that you wish to encourage.

■ Thrifty

Everything in the world, whether it is emotional, physical or financial, has a cost, and the cost is paid somewhere by someone. Good negotiators never forget that. All the 'free offers' you see in the shops are being paid for out of the profits that are made from the rest of the goods on sale.

Whenever you are negotiating you have a finite amount of assets available to trade. The more you get in return for your assets, the more you have available for tomorrow's deal. And you never know how much the context will change. Something given away today may be worth a fortune tomorrow. Conversely you may feel rich today because your shares are worth a fortune and find yourself shockingly impoverished a week later after a stock market crash. An extravagant gesture today may be more than you can afford in a week's time.

Negotiators who have seen their markets rise and fall a few times learn to be economical. When times are hard a negotiator with a bit of spare cash can pick up wonderful bargains. Inexperienced negotiators sometimes worry that they are being mean or ungenerous. If they get the keenest price possible in a deal, are they being too hard on the other party?

Experience teaches us that in many ways negotiation produces a sense of equity more effectively than generosity. There is no way to ensure that the recipient of a gift is grateful or has any sense that they should reciprocate. Negotiation, by contrast, makes mutual obligations explicit. Hence negotiation is more reliable in promoting social support and interdependence than generosity.

People almost invariably value what they pay for above what is given to them for free. By earning their side of the bargain, people tend to feel they are entitled to it by virtue of their own efforts. By contrast, recipients of generosity forget it far more quickly. Interestingly they are typically less appreciative of what they get and less happy with it too.

This is not to say that wealthy negotiators are never generous. They may well be generous and charitable but they do not mix charity and negotiation. It is both difficult and hazardous to be unilaterally generous in a business deal. It is far easier to stay businesslike throughout your negotiation. If you really want to give someone a present, do so entirely separately from the negotiation after it is concluded. You may by that time realize that they are doing well enough out of the deal not to need your generosity.

■ Goal-orientated

Negotiators are goal-orientated. They like making things happen. They have a bias towards action. They are willing to make connections, to make the first move, to pick up a telephone and ask a question. Often the difference between success and failure is as small as the difference between saying hello and just nodding and passing by. Negotiators tend to say hello. They ask questions and when they see a possibility they set their sights on it.

An amazing number of good deals happen because a chance meeting reveals a vital piece of information. Once the possibility of a deal is formed in a negotiator's mind they begin to work towards it.

After talking to his friend at ABC Duncan had lunch with Ivor. Ivor has very good connections with a South American government and he happened to mention that they were trying to get the jet fighters in their air force upgraded. They were also looking into establishing a national airline. All of a sudden, Duncan saw the possibility of a deal.

ABC needed to find some offset expenditure to introduce to the Balkans. The South Americans needed their fighters upgraded. If the South American contact was introduced to the Balkans, ABC would get their offset. But why would the South Americans assist ABC? They wanted some passenger aircraft for their airline. ABC had an aviation division which had some suitable aircraft. If Duncan's firm leased them from ABC and provided them to the South Americans they would get their airline in return for choosing the Balkan company to upgrade their fighters. Duncan saw his goal and got down to work.

Duncan's deal had several parties and several million pounds involved, but goals don't have to be grand and deals don't have to be complex. The same principles of curiosity, awareness, solution-focus and goal-orientation can work in very small-scale settings.

Scott Miller is a therapist who trained with Steve de Shazer and he is fond of using goal-setting as a therapeutic intervention. He once asked a very depressed woman with an alcohol problem what would be the smallest sign she could think of that therapy was working for her.

'I guess,' she told him, 'I'd make the effort to brush my hair nicely.'

'That sounds like a great place to start,' said Scott. 'I look forward to seeing whether that has happened when we meet again.'

The following week his client had not only brushed her hair, she had put on some make-up as well. A few months later she had made astonishing progress.

A goal provides a focus for our energy and our attention. If you bear in mind where you want to get to then you scan whatever you come across in terms of how it can help you. As Paul McKenna says, 'You always get more of what you focus on.'

Goal-setting also ensures that your activities are structured by what you are moving towards rather than what you are moving away from. If I just want to get away from something no direction is necessarily any better than any other. If I am dissatisfied with my job, complaining about it won't make any useful difference. Wanting to leave doesn't give me any indication of where I should go. It is easier to find out what I want to move towards.

I need to decide what sort of things will make me feel better. Would more money improve my mood? If so, I set a goal of negotiating a better salary. Now I have something specific to move towards. Would it be more fun to work in a different team? Would a better desk, a better title or a better office make me feel better? If the answer is yes to any of these, I have a positive goal to work towards.

Do I want to change jobs? If so, I must specify what sort of job I want. Where do I want to work? What do I want to do? What hours would I prefer? My search for a new job will be much more efficient when I know at least some of the characteristics I am looking for. This remains true even if during the search some of my criteria change. It helps because setting goals creates a positive frame of *moving towards* something.

We will see in the next chapter how important it is to set specific goals for your negotiation, but there is no need to wait for a negotiation opportunity to crop up to practise setting goals.

But what if you only know what you don't want? Every negative desire actually refers to a positive. We only experience something as negative or unpleasant because we can conceive of something we would prefer, in other words something better. If we didn't have that positive desire we would not experience any dissatisfaction. For example, you might want your neighbour to stop playing his loud and repetitive rock music. In other words, you don't want to hear it. The positive desire behind this is that you want to enjoy the experience of quietness. When you open negotiations with your neighbour you will find it a lot easier when you concentrate on what you do want rather than think or say negative things about what you don't want. The chances are that your neighbour will find it easier to negotiate with you like that too.

■ GOAL SETTING

- ■ Set clear goals.
- ■ Break down bigger goals into a series of smaller ones.
- ■ Always frame your goals in terms of what you wish to move towards, not as moving away.

■ Tough

It is advantageous to appear tough in negotiation, but being tough in negotiation is not the same as being aggressive. You don't have to be threatening or intimidating. The essence of toughness is simply standing your ground. Three ideas will help you appear tough in negotiation. First, don't take anything the other party says personally. Remember they are negotiating about a deal, not about your status in society. They are not authorized to be a judge of your character; they are simply trying to do a deal.

Secondly, be very clear about what you want out of the deal. Focus your attention and your speech on what you are trying to achieve, not on comments about your character or the other person's. One of the most powerful responses to any comment on your situation or character is simply to ignore it. The best way to do that is to return to the actual topic of the negotiation.

Thirdly, the action that most clearly demonstrates your toughness is making sure that any offer you make to the other party involves the smallest feasible move from your position towards theirs and the largest feasible move by them towards you. When we look at specific techniques we will see many ways to do this. At this stage we can just note that negotiation does not entail both parties making equal moves towards each other. It only entails moving as far as necessary to secure a deal that both sides are happy to agree to.

You may not have to move very far at all in order to secure agreement, and the less you move the greater the impression that the other party needs to move more towards you.

You may in fact be the kindest, sweetest person in the country. You can stay kind and sweet and yet be tough in negotiation because being tough does not entail turning into a rhinoceros-hide monster. It is a matter of appearing tough to the other party by sticking to your negotiation agenda. Toughness is simply valuing your own input into the deal highly so that you give away as little as possible.

Is it necessary to be tough? Yes. Your attitude has a direct effect on that of the other party. The best reason for being tough is that more often than not it elicits a conciliatory response in the other party. The tougher you are, the more they try to appease you. While aggressiveness evokes defensiveness, toughness evokes softness.

▓ Persistent

One point that all negotiators agree on is that persistence pays off. Just keep going. Persistence, like a lot else in negotiation, is essentially simple. If at first you don't succeed, try again. And again. And again until you do succeed.

The only caveat is to be sure that you are persistent in pursuit of your ultimate aim, not persistently attached to one particular way of achieving it. If you have set clear goals and you can check that none of your ethics will be violated, it really doesn't matter how you get what you want.

Persistence is remarkably powerful.

In 1967, Father James Horan became the priest of the parish of Knock, in Ireland. Knock had a shrine to the Virgin Mary, and Father James believed it deserved a better church than the one he inherited. By 1976, Knock had a church covering an acre of ground that could accommodate 10,000 people. In 1979, the centenary of the visions that were the reason for the shrine's existence, Father James persuaded the Pope to visit Knock.

After that, Father James, not content with an enormous new church and a papal visit, decided the shrine at Knock deserved an international airport. There was at the time no economic argument for an airport capable of receiving jumbo jets in County Mayo, a rural and sparsely populated area in the west of Ireland, but Father James was nothing if not persistent.

He extracted a promise of millions of pounds from the Irish government, and when the government changed and the funding stopped, he raised money from the local community, from the Irish abroad and from the European Community. The first flight took off from Knock airport in 1985. Few negotiators could match Father James Horan for political or negotiation skills, and above all else he was irrepressibly, unstoppably persistent.

Most negotiators have discovered by trial and error that persistence works. They have learned to stick at it because they know it pays off. But behind that simple truth was another one. In each case their persistence was founded in a strong and clear connection to their values. They knew what they wanted. And even more than that, they knew why they wanted it.

Knowing what you want, and why you want it, is far more important than knowing how, where or when you are going to get it. When you know what and why, all the rest will eventually follow.

The more you persist, the more you learn about patterns of progress. You will find that very often indeed you come across obstacles on the path to your goal. You have to revise your plans, add more resources and put in extra effort. That is just the way of the world. Very little that is worth achieving comes easily. By the same token, it is through the effort you put in that you earn the sense of achievement when you succeed.

IMAGINE YOUR DESIRED OUTCOME

- When the going gets too tough a neat way to keep your spirits up is to vividly imagine the wonderful feeling you will have when you achieve your goal. Picture a specific rewarding situation that will occur when you have succeeded.

For example, writing this book has been a long process with lots of ups and downs as I tried various different ways of explaining things. There were plenty of dead ends and wrong turnings on the way, and from time to time I felt worried and dissatisfied. Dissatisfaction was actually useful in helping me to raise my standards. Worries, however, were debilitating, so I replaced them with anticipation. I regularly imagined holding the finished book in my hand and the sense of satisfaction I would have when I had completed the job. If I wanted to feel even better, I imagined having a party where I met all the friends I didn't have time to see while I was writing.

▓ Realistic

To see the world realistically means to see what is feasible. It is not the same as knowing what is normal or probable. If we only ever achieved what was most probable no one would ever win a game of roulette, no lottery prize would ever be claimed and no Olympic medals would ever be won by anyone.

In reality, people routinely achieve improbable feats. What are these people like? They are realistic. Olympic medal winners don't train once a week, they train every day for years.

Negotiators are realistic in that they make sure that each step of their proposals is feasible. They may from time to time suggest something a little wild as a negotiating ploy, but when they get down to the agreement they want to know it works, so realism is vital.

Being realistic means that you don't expect to buy a house advertised at £200,000 for £50,000. But if the opportunity arises you jump at it. In 1997 the Thai economy, having enjoyed a credit-led boom, collapsed and high-living Thais suddenly ran out of money. Thousands of people had to put their luxury goods up for sale and for a short period of time you could buy an almost-new Mercedes for the equivalent of just a few hundred pounds. A lot of quick-thinking negotiators all over Asia filled their wallets with cash and jumped on a plane to Thailand.

▓ Confident

The funny thing about confidence is that when you've got it, you don't think about it. And although we have the phrase 'lack of confidence', it would be more accurate to talk about 'presence of misunderstanding'. Confidence is a basic human capacity. Lack of confidence is really the result of being misled and distracted by worries and negative beliefs. Confidence arises from a healthy awareness of the competence of your unconscious mind. It is our natural state. It is only the peculiar standards and activities of our society that cause us to get cut off from it.

If you watch a baby learning to walk you will see that it takes a long time crawling, then holding on to things while it stands up, and then tottering across the room before it can really walk. And while it is learning it falls over, again and again and again. Sometimes it even hurts itself. But again and again and again it gets up and tries once more. A baby has a natural, in-built confidence that keeps it trying until it eventually succeeds. Babies learn to walk before they learn to talk. It is not because someone has told them it will happen that they are confident. All that persistent confidence comes from the inside. That same confidence is hard-wired into all of us. As adults we just need to get back in touch with it.

Lack of confidence arises when we don't trust ourselves, which essentially means not trusting the unconscious. At any one time, 99 per cent of all your knowledge, insight and abilities is stored in the unconscious mind. Your ability to react, your intelligence, your perception, your memory – in fact, all your physical, intellectual and emotional capacities are maintained by your unconscious mind. Your mind is like an iceberg – the vast majority of it is hidden and only a tiny part, your conscious attention, is visible above the surface.

The biggest cause of lack of confidence is people being unaware of the constant support of the unconscious. They believe that they have to do everything with their conscious awareness. That is very hard work.

Do you type? Have you noticed that when you think about where the letters are it slows you down? Have you noticed how difficult it is to tie your shoelaces when you think about it? It is quicker just to let your hands get on with it. When you have learned a skill well, your unconscious refines it over and over again. You find that you do it better and quicker when your conscious mind keeps out of the way.

Confidence is not certainty. It is the willingness to act in the face of uncertainty. And that is something we do nearly all the time, because when you really look around in life, everything is uncertain, but we get on with it.

Your confidence increases naturally the more you negotiate, but there are lots of other ways to reconnect to it. If you are the methodical sort, or you simply want a quick strong fix right now, then you can use the techniques and exercises below.

The mind and body are completely interconnected.[5] All our feelings are registered in our bodies and everything we do with our bodies affects how we feel. Many of these feelings and responses are fleeting and subtle, but powerful enduring postures create enduring feelings, and strong feelings have a measurable physiological effect. For example, depressed people tend to move slowly, they look downwards, their shoulders slump and they have a sad or bored expression on their face. If you did all that for a long period of time you would feel depressed. So don't.

On the other hand, happy people tend to smile a lot, their movements are lively and they are more likely to walk tall, to look you in the eye and be alert to whatever is going on around them. They carry less tension in their bodies and are consequently healthier too. Happier people are also more likely to score highly on optimism and confidence tests.

GOLDEN THREAD

One of the simplest, easiest ways to increase your confidence is to reduce the tension in your body.

- Sit or stand in a more upright posture and relax your face.
- Imagine a golden thread is running up from the base of your spine through the centre of your head and all the way up to the sky.
- Imagine yourself supported by that thread, with no effort at all.
- Let the thread keep you upright while you let the tension fall out of your shoulders, face and neck.

Smiling increases your confidence and your happiness. There are two sorts of smile, a real one and a forced one. By far the most powerful and rewarding is the real one. Smiling is an autonomous process mediated by the unconscious mind. So to put a genuine smile on your face, don't force it, but simply imagine that you are smiling. Feel a smile inside yourself. Remember a person or situation that made you smile and notice the feeling you experience. When you do that the muscles that move in your face are moved by your unconscious, just as they are in a real smile. It may not be a big wide smile but it is genuine because it is your body's autonomous response to your inner feeling.

■ CONFIDENCE GYM

Some people like to use specific exercises to develop their psychological capacities. These are the psychological equivalent of going to the gym. Here is a confidence-boosting exercise from the 'psychological gym'. It makes use of the fact that your body reacts in the same way to vividly imagined or remembered experience as it does to real life.

- Remember a time when you felt really confident. You can choose any time at all, from any time of your life. It doesn't matter whether the incident was significant or trivial or whether anyone else noticed at the time. Just pick a time when you really felt confident.
- Now make a little video clip of that time in your imagination. Imagine seeing yourself being confident. Notice your situation. Notice what you can see around you. Have a good look at that video clip and fill in as many details as you can.
- Now imagine stepping into yourself in that memory, so that you see through your own eyes, hear what you heard and feel what you felt. Look around your own experience and make everything vivid. See the colours bright and clear, and make the focus sharp. Hear every sound around you exactly and notice everything that you feel.
- Notice the temperature and the feeling of your skin.
- Notice the feelings of confidence inside you.
- Pay very close attention to exactly how confidence feels for you.
- Intensify that feeling by making your experience more and more vivid.
- When you feel a strong, comfortable feeling of confidence, press the finger and thumb of one hand together.
- Do this over and over again. You can use lots of different memories of

confidence, or you can use the same one over and over again. All that matters is that each time you make the memory so vivid that you actually feel the feeling of confidence in your body and when you feel it nice and strong you press together your finger and thumb.

■ Practise this exercise for at least three minutes every day for two weeks, and you will find that just thinking about confidence and pressing your finger and thumb together will bring those feelings of confidence flooding into you.

I've taught this exercise to all sorts of people, and a good number of them look very cynical when I first describe it to them. There is often a sense that it is vaguely ridiculous to make pretty pictures in your mind and play around with associations. But whatever you think of it, you have nothing to lose, at most three minutes a day of your time. So if you think you'd like to be more aware of your confidence, try it.

In the end, it doesn't matter how you connect to your confidence. Once you are used to it, it becomes a natural part of your being again, just as it was when you first learned to walk. And then you are free to focus the whole of your mind on exploring the world again, just as you did when you finally stood on your own two feet and set off on your own.

■ Sociable

Negotiation is a conversation that leads to agreement. It follows that good negotiators enjoy a good conversation. They enjoy meeting people and they enjoy talking to them.

Sociability is a natural human trait. Human beings are herd animals who need to cooperate to survive. We learn to talk through spontaneous, automatic interaction with other humans. There are all sorts of reasons why some of us lose touch with this natural ability. Some people are brought up in circumstances which inhibit sociability. Others have specific experiences which teach them to become shy or diffident, and all of us can choose from time to time to withdraw a little to spend time on our own.

Being a negotiator means you always have something to talk about.

If you aren't doing a deal now, there is one you've just completed and another one in the offing, and who knows maybe yet another one will begin to emerge during this very conversation.

You don't have to make meaningless small talk. On the contrary, sociability is a way of finding out what people are interested in and a way to satisfy your own curiosity. Use the suggestions below if you would like to restore your natural ability to be sociable.

▐ INCREASE YOUR SOCIABILITY

- Set yourself the task of talking to one stranger a day. You will notice that it's often easier to meet people when you are not in places where talking to other people is expected or intended. It is far easier to talk to a stranger in a supermarket queue than at a bar. It is easier for a man to talk to a woman in a shop than in a nightclub, and it is easier for a woman to approach a man almost anywhere other than a pub or a club.
- Ask for help. If you find the idea of talking to strangers a little intimidating, you can start just by asking for the time. When you are used to that you could ask other questions.
- Ask 'open' questions. An open question is one to which the answer cannot be 'yes' or 'no'. For example, 'Did you come here by train?' is a closed question because you can answer it with just 'yes' or 'no'. The question, 'How did you get here?' is an open question. Whatever the answer, it is an opportunity to carry on the conversation about the details of whichever method was used.
- Be polite. Make a point of thanking people who give you good service, whether in shops, trains or aeroplanes. If you help people, whether offering a seat to an elderly person on a train or holding open a door for a mum with a pushchair, you will find you can easily exchange a few words them as you do so.
- Remember that every person in the world has a unique point of view. Find out what makes each person special. If you meet someone just once, this is your chance to find out what it is that only they know. Take that chance!

■ Relaxed

The French have a wonderful expression for someone who is at ease with themselves. They say that you are '*bien dans ta peau*', meaning 'comfortable in your skin'. Being able to feel comfortable in your skin wherever you are is a particularly useful attribute. You will often find yourself going into new situations to deal with other negotiators. That might mean travelling halfway around the world or it might mean crossing to the other side of town.

You might have to do business with people who are less well off than you. When you are happy in yourself you will be neither patronizing nor judgemental. If they wish to increase their wealth, your business may enable them to do so. If they are happy with their level of wealth, they are probably a lot happier than someone obsessed with money. You might find yourself visiting houses of the super-wealthy where the doors are opened by servants, or entering the world of big business where reception areas are designed to intimidate and boardrooms are decorated with ostentatiously expensive works of art.

A good negotiator takes it all in her stride. She doesn't ignore it, she enjoys it. If you find yourself in surroundings far more opulent than you are used to, enjoy it, but don't take it too seriously.

There are only three reasons why people spend huge sums of money on their surroundings.

The first is that they don't really care how much things cost because they have so much money that price tags are meaningless. If that is the case, there is no reason for you to pay any attention to the price tag either.

The second reason is that, regardless of the cost, they absolutely love the space they have created and were willing to spend what it took. If someone cares that much about their environment, there is probably something for you to enjoy about it too. And if you don't like it, you can always marvel at the extraordinary range of taste that is found in the human race.

The third reason people spend huge sums on luxury goods and interior design is that they want to impress you. They want you to know how rich they are. If that is the case, you should take it as a compliment that they have so much respect for your potential that they feel the need to impress you. Either that or wonder in what way they are so insecure as to need to spend so much money on bolstering their image.

■ MAKE YOURSELF FEEL AT EASE

Being at ease in any situation is closely related to confidence. You can use the Confidence Gym on pages 52–3 or the Golden Thread technique on page 51 to get in touch with your confidence whenever you need it. You can feel comfortable anywhere in the world when you bring your comfort with you. Here is an easy visualization technique to make that feeling available wherever you are.

- Get comfortable right now. Stretch your limbs and then relax them. Feel that golden thread from the sky supporting you (see page 51).
- Breathe out all the way to the bottom of your lungs and then let a clean, deep breath of fresh air revitalize you.
- Notice how your breath carries on by itself and your heart beats by itself. Relax and let yourself be carried by the force of life within you.
- Notice how effortless it is.
- Take all the time you need to enjoy this feeling of relaxation and ease, and feel it throughout your body.
- Now imagine that the feeling has a colour, and in your mind's eye imagine your whole body gradually coloured more and more brightly with that colour as you feel relaxed, confident, alert and ready to deal with anyone you meet.
- Enjoy this feeling as long as you want, and keep visualizing the colour as you keep your awareness of this comfortable feeling throughout your body.
- When you feel as comfortable as you could possibly want to, keep the feeling and let the colour soak away into you like water sinking into the sand on a beach.
- Next time you want to feel completely at ease, imagine that feeling-colour being poured into your body and filling you up from your feet upwards. At first your feet are full of comfort and confidence, then it rises up your legs to your knees, then your thighs and waist. Then it fills your abdomen, rises up in your chest and runs down your arms to your hands before filling up your shoulders, neck and head.

As we saw earlier, however strange this visualization may seem to your intellect, it is a very powerful way of communicating with your feelings and your body. Your body does not react to words or ideas. It reacts to vividly imagined pictures.

At ease with money

Money is not an absolute measure of value. It is a means of translating value, and the price of anything at any time is determined by the buyer, the seller and the context.

The phenomenon of fixed prices has given rise to the illusion that prices are somehow independent of buyers. It is true that for the sake of convenience much of the time we pay the price shown on the tag, but if not enough people are willing to do so, what happens? The shop has a sale and changes the price on the tag. Our collective lack of willingness to buy forces the price down.

Prices are not fixed, and money is not a measure of your value. However, money often reflects how you value yourself. I have often come across situations where people needed to raise their prices in order to get more business. Customers are suspicious of people who charge markedly less than the standard rate in the market. In the absence of other information, a low price can imply poor quality or a substandard product.

In some cultures there is a tradition of avoiding talking about money. If you come from such a background, practise the mirror exercise below.

Many of my negotiation clients are some of the millions of people who have started their own businesses in the last decade. The vast majority of these people are sole traders. They have moved from the cosy world of spending the boss's money and receiving a regular salary at the end of the month to the harsh world where the boss's money is their own and there is no money at all until the customer pays. One of the commonest problems in the early days of a business is failing to charge enough for its products or services.

In particular, people who have left jobs they dislike to pursue a vocation they love such as being an artist, a therapist or a performer often tell me they feel guilty about charging for their services because they love their job. I like to remind them that I would rather receive the services of someone who loves what they are doing than someone who is only doing it for the money. Furthermore, if you enjoy doing it the chances are that you will be doing it better than the competition, so you should be charging *more* than other people.

BEING AT EASE WITH MONEY

If you are convinced that you should charge more, but are still shy about naming your price, use this exercise.

- Stand in front of a mirror and think of a sum of money you feel comfortable charging. For example, £50.
- Looking at yourself in the mirror, say out loud, 'That costs £70.'
- Check how you feel. If you feel at all nervous or worried reduce the amount until you feel completely at ease saying, 'I charge £50.'
- Looking yourself in the eye, repeat that phrase over and over again until you can say it without any worries at all.
- Now increase the sum by 20 per cent, and repeat the sentence. For example, 'That costs £60.'
- Once again repeat it and keep repeating it until you get used to the sound of it and used to the idea of it and you feel entirely comfortable saying, 'I charge £60.'
- When you feel at ease with that price, increase it by another 20 per cent and repeat the whole process. For example, 'I charge £72.'
- Continue saying that until you feel completely at ease naming this price.
- Now increase the price once more, and do it again. Carry on increasing the price and repeating it in the mirror until the price you mention is at the top of the range of prices in your market.

Flexible

A good negotiator sets goals, but he doesn't set them in concrete. He is flexible. He is flexible about what he gets and how he gets it, provided he focuses on the ultimate values he is attempting to satisfy.

In the 1980s Stuart and Neil spotted an anomaly in the world oil-tanker market. There were more tankers than there was business to fill them, so they were cheap to buy and no one was building new ones. However, the vast majority of the ships in the marketplace were nearing the end of their working lives and within three or four years they would have to be scrapped. Stuart and Neil realized that they could buy nearly new tankers relatively cheaply and in a few years they would be worth vastly more. They raised the necessary money and bought half a dozen nearly new very large tankers.

Then, suddenly and unexpectedly, the oil market picked up. There were not enough tankers available to make all the shipments that were being ordered and charter rates went through the roof. Stuart and Neil found themselves operating an unexpectedly lucrative business, so they abandoned their original plan to sell on their tankers and ran a shipping business successfully for several years before selling it for a considerable sum. The initial plan had been to make money, and that is what they did, but they were flexible enough to see that it could come from an unexpected direction.

INCREASE YOUR FLEXIBILITY

- Remember there are always other options. All that is necessary to increase your flexibility is to remember that there are more ways than one to achieve your goals.
- Ask yourself: If I knew I could not fail, how many different ways could I achieve my goals?
- Sometimes a goal you set yourself becomes unattainable. The item you wanted to buy has been sold, or you cannot afford the price asked and the vendor refuses to come down. If that happens, ask yourself: What would I have felt and what would I have got if I'd achieved my original goal? In other words, what would achieving your original goal have done for you? These questions help you to establish your internal motivation.
- When you have clarified your internal motivation, ask yourself: How many other ways can I think of to satisfy this? Find at least two different ways to satisfy your internal motivation.
- Use one of those ways to define your next goal.

■ Persuasive

Negotiation is often thought of as trading one thing for another. Before that can happen, however, it is necessary to persuade the other party that they want to trade.

A good negotiator must be persuasive. He needs to engage the other party's interest and then persuade them of the attractiveness of his proposal. If the persuasion is powerful enough, the other party may accept your first offer. Better still, sometimes people will simply give you what want without asking for anything in return.

Persuasion can do a huge amount of the work of negotiation. The more persuasive you are, the less you need to give. Your goal in negotiation is to get what you want and at the same time to persuade the other party that they want what they get.

The essence of persuasion is belief. When you truly believe in the value of your proposal, you release your natural enthusiasm. That is a wonderful basis for negotiation and encourages the other party to become enthusiastic and committed too. When you genuinely believe in your proposal, simple words are just as persuasive as the most eloquent arguments.

We will look at specific techniques of persuasion in Chapter 5. Here I will just mention three general principles of persuasion in negotiation.

First, persuasion is not a matter of argument, it is a matter of sentiment. Arguing with people is absolutely the hardest way to change their minds because it tends to make them defend their beliefs and become more attached to them. The easiest way to persuade is through the heart, not the head. When someone is emotionally committed to something, they will find rational reasons to justify their decision. If you let them find something they are attracted to about your proposition, they will find their own reasons to underpin their emotional decision.

Secondly, your goal is to persuade the other party to accept your offer, not to agree with you about its merits. Remember to let each person agree with you on their own grounds.

Thirdly, almost all persuasion relies on having an understanding of the other party's point of view. If you can see what the situation looks like to them, you will also see what will be attractive to them.

■ INCREASE YOUR PERSUASIVENESS

- Believe in your offer.
- Find something likeable in the person with whom you are negotiating and remember it when you talk to them.
- Find out what the other party finds attractive in your offer and empha size that. Don't talk about what *you* think is important, talk about what *they* think is important.

■ Authentic

We have been through quite a list of the characteristics of the successful negotiator. You might be thinking that some of them are more familiar to you than others. You might be unsure that you would ever be able to describe yourself like this, yet all of these characteristics are attainable by all of us. We can all be optimistic, curious, aware, solution-focused, thrifty, goal-orientated, tough, persistent, realistic, confident, sociable, relaxed, at ease with money, flexible and persuasive.

However, importantly, although we have so much in common, we all have our own unique characters. Good negotiators are always true to themselves.

It is helpful to think of ourselves as having a combination of two ways of being. All of us have learned how to 'join in' with the human race. We learn the language of our community and the traditions and behaviour of our family. We didn't choose the language – it was there before us and it will be there after us. So this part of our life we can call 'life in common'. But each of us has a unique point of view. You are the only person living your life, so as well as all that you have in common with the rest of us, you also have your unique position, understanding and possibilities.

When you learn to negotiate, you are adding more to what you have in common with other good negotiators, but you do it from your own unique position and your own point of view. Through negotiation you can add more to your own life and assert your own values more and more. Changing your way of being like this is not a matter of limiting yourself – but rather a matter of expanding and extending your own possibilities.

So, when you practise these techniques and explore these characteristics, don't try to be someone else. Find the seed of your own confidence and let it grow. Find your own way to be sociable and optimistic, find your own expression of solution-focused thinking, flexibility, persuasiveness and so forth. You will find them all by experimenting. Try each of them out in any context whatsoever, and see what happens. Negotiations, like romance, can happen anywhere. So you can be prepared by starting right now.

Being true to yourself is both powerful and valuable. Instinctively, we all scan each other's non-verbal communications, such as posture, intonation, timing, eye contact and so forth, in order to decide how much to trust each other. When you speak from your true feelings and beliefs, all your non-verbal signals are congruent with your words, which means you are more likely to be understood and trusted. This is why statements from the heart have such a strong impact. Being authentic does not demand that you tell the entire truth about a situation (even if that were possible) – it simply means making sure you never contradict what you really feel and believe.

The chief executive of a large municipal corporation had called in an arbitration service to negotiate the settlement of a strike. The arbitration protocol is for the two parties in a dispute to sit in separate rooms while the negotiator goes from one to the other as he or she brokers the deal.

On this occasion the negotiator spent ten minutes with the management team and then nearly six hours with the unions. As time passed the management team became more and more uneasy and more and more annoyed. They were convinced that the negotiator was becoming far too close to the unions and was going to present them with a stitch-up. They weren't even sure that he was doing his job properly as his time allocation was scarcely even-handed. When he finally reappeared they told him what they thought.

All of a sudden the arbitrator lost his temper. 'You've no bloody idea!' he told them. 'We haven't been ganging up on you. I've been spend all that time trying to get three different unions to stay in the same room long enough to agree what they want to ask for!'

His honest expression of his exasperation probably wasn't in his rulebook, but its authenticity re-established the trust of the management in his behaviour.

■ BEING AUTHENTIC

- ■ Before any important statement or decision, listen to your own emotional intelligence. This is best done by paying attention to the whole of your body, and noticing in particular what you feel in your solar plexus. Try to put your own feelings into words to yourself, and check that they are congruent with the position you are taking in the negotiation.
- ■ If you are honest with yourself it is hard for other people to manipulate you. If you are prepared to notice, and admit, what you are feeling – for example, full of pride, or hurt – you are less likely to be outmanoeuvred by someone who deliberately flatters or riles you.

■ Powerful

Money, beauty, property, strength, intelligence, knowledge, skills and status are all sources of power. But most of all, power is in the eye of the beholder. You don't need to be endowed with preternatural amounts of any of these talents or possessions to be a powerful negotiator.

In negotiation both parties always have some power. If one party had all the power they would not need to negotiate, they could simply command. How the power is distributed in the negotiation can change radically, and ultimately the greater part of power is the perception of power. If someone believes you are powerful, then you are.

All the personal qualities we have been looking at in this section are sources of power. In the most artful negotiations power is not used overtly at all. Instead proposals are offered in terms of the advantages they offer and the pressures on the other party are not mentioned. This has the advantage of making future rapport and negotiation easier because all parties can remain friendly and respectful.

But perhaps the greatest form of power is so subtle it is almost invisible. Richard Elkin is an American therapist working with families. He tells a story from a time in his youth when he practised a great deal of karate and had obtained a black belt. He was on a subway train one evening and a large, leery, drunken man got on board clutching a bottle in a brown paper bag. He looked like trouble. Mentally Richard prepared himself to tackle him if he started harassing any of the women on the train. He was just deciding whether to kick him first or punch him, when a high-pitched Japanese voice sang out, 'Hey, mister, what you drinking?'

The drunk swung round to see a little old Japanese man smiling at him.

'I'm drinking bourbon,' snarled the drunk, lurching over towards him.

'Sit with me,' said the Japanese man, patting the seat next to him. 'I like to drink sake. I drink it with my wife. Do you drink with your wife?'

The drunk collapsed like a burst balloon. 'She's left me,' he wailed.

The Japanese man patted his arm and talked to him.

As Richard observed later, the old man was the real karate master.

Power takes many forms and can be exercised in many ways. The peril posed by power is that it can be used to boost the ego. People who use it in that way are no longer truly powerful, but rather power addicts who need to continue displaying their power in order to feel good. A good negotiator remembers that his goal is not an ego massage but a deal, so he uses his power sparingly and only displays it nakedly if absolutely necessary.

Some of the most ethical uses of power are almost invisible. The Japanese man's negotiation with the belligerence of the drunk avoided confrontation and elegantly offered him the opportunity to talk about his troubles.

▌ INCREASE YOUR POWER

- ▪ Power comes from the inside. It comes from developing all the attributes we have been exploring in this chapter.
- ▪ Don't try too hard. The greatest power is not the loudest but the most enduring. Your goal should be to achieve your aim with the minimum overt use of power. True power is all the more powerful for being discreet.

▌ A good listener

The Japanese gentleman also demonstrated his remarkable skills as a listener. Not only did he listen to the drunk's tale of woe, but he heard the distress that was there beneath his drunken bravado as soon as he got on the train.

True, deep listening is an invaluable skill and one that a negotiator continually exercises and renews. In the commercial context one needs to be alert for any hint of further information that may affect your deal.

When you are making offers and hearing counter-offers make sure that you really hear what the other person is saying. In business, money focuses the mind, but it can focus it too narrowly. Make sure you hear everything that is being said, not just the sums of money mentioned. Pay attention to all that is said and be wary of assuming that you understand what it means. For example, when you look at a house, ask lots of questions and listen very carefully to the replies. If the vendors tell you that they get on well with their neighbours, ask what they do together. If they enjoy sitting down to belt out rock and roll numbers all night long, you might think twice about buying the house.

In personal and emotional negotiations, listening is equally important, and even more so if we think we already know what the problem is. All too often we hear what we want to hear and we see what we want to see.

In family and relationship circumstances, emotional issues can provoke powerful responses that distract you. Make sure you identify any such responses so that you are not carried away by them.

BEING A GOOD LISTENER

- If in doubt, don't talk, listen. Listening openly, with compassion, is in itself a positive action. Many problems in relationships arise because someone feels ignored. Listening hard, without prejudice, might be the solution your partner is looking for.
- Play it back. If there is any danger of emotions running high, it is good to set up a protocol of repeating back the offer to check you have heard it correctly. If, at the beginning, you set up the habit of repeating what you have heard for the purposes of clarification, the other party will be able to correct any misunderstanding.
- Remember there is always more to learn. Keep listening. Many deals are made or broken on the basis of information that comes out at the last moment. To hear it, you've got to be listening.

Don't make life
complicated
when something simple
will do

Chapter 3
Setting up a deal

❑ Evaluate the opportunity

❑ Know what you want

❑ Asking what-if questions

❑ Understanding the other party

❑ What's the alternative to the deal?

What are you going to negotiate? Are you trying to buy a house? Set up a business? Bring about a family reconciliation? Whatever you want to negotiate, preparation will be a vital part of your success. In this chapter we will look at all the elements of preparation before you start negotiating.

Of course, there are situations in which you don't have time to set up a deal, you just have to negotiate immediately. If so, all you have learned about the way of being of a negotiator will stand you in good stead. But in the conversation of negotiation, don't forget that you can do much of what follows while negotiating.

■ The beginning

Negotiations start as soon as you scent the possibility of a deal. That is often long before you start talking to the other party or parties involved. As a negotiator you will now tend to be curious about the contexts in which you find yourself, and being solution-focused and goal-orientated all sorts of opportunities will appear to you. Generally speaking, your best deals will be the ones that spring from opportunities that other people have not noticed. If you are the first person to make the connections, you have first-mover advantage.

Golden opportunities are as rare as gold, but that need not inhibit you. There are plenty of useful deals to be done to keep you ticking over. And in the non-financial world there is an unending supply of issues that will be greatly improved by the intelligent application of your negotiation skills. However, in choosing your deals, remember to bear in mind your own capacity. Negotiation requires your full attention so don't spread it too thin.

Of course, there are occasions when you have not *chosen* to negotiate, it is just your least worst option in the circumstances. If you have been stopped for speeding, for example, you have nothing to lose and a lot to gain if you persuade the policeman to accept your apologies and your explanation.

It is not always possible to do all your preparation in advance, but the more you have ready, the better. In any case, much of it should be continued throughout the process. You start gathering information as soon as the idea of the deal forms in your mind, but you carry on collecting information and monitoring the situation all the way through until the deal is signed.

Just ask

Don't do something complicated when something simple will do. Sometimes you don't need to get into negotiations at all. Sometimes you can get what you want by just asking.

I have developed a habit of asking for a discount whenever I go shopping. Often I didn't need to do any more than that to be offered a reduction in the price. I took a book of sheet music to the sales assistant, showed her a tear on one page and asked for a 10 per cent discount. She gave me the discount, and then rounded it down to the nearest pound. But you don't need to find a flaw in a product to ask for a discount. In another shop I found a pair of jeans I liked but I thought the price was outrageous, and I told the salesman so. 'I can give you ten pounds off,' he replied. That was before I had asked for anything. I had just commented on how high his prices were. So then I asked him for another ten pounds off. He agreed. As things were going so well, I asked for yet another ten pounds off. That he wouldn't do, but as the price of the jeans had by now been reduced by twenty pounds I was happy to buy them.

If you don't ask, you don't get. Sometimes just asking does the trick. Other times your request opens a conversation, and in the conversation you can start to negotiate.

Twice as powerful

You will be delighted to hear that there is a way to make asking even more effective. In an intriguing experiment in the 1970s, Ellen Langer and her colleagues tested the effectiveness of different ways of asking a favour. Ellen asked some people queueing to use a photocopier if she could use the machine ahead of them. Sixty per cent of them agreed to let her. In other words, just asking got her what she wanted more than half the time.

However, she found a way to increase compliance by more than 50 per cent. She asked the same question, but added a reason: 'Because I'm in a rush.' When she added the reason, 94 per cent of the people agreed to let her go in front of them.

Offering people a reason for your request massively increases the chances of compliance. But Ellen's experiment produced another important finding.

She made the same request of some more people in the same situation but gave a different reason: 'Because I have to make some copies.' When she did that she achieved virtually the same rate of compliance – 93 per cent. Her 'reason' was scarcely a reason at all. It gave no more information; it just restated what was obvious but in a sentence using the word 'because'. Yet it had almost the same effect.

Using reasons, or words that sound like reasons, is a very persuasive way to increase the effectiveness of your requests.

■ Choosing a deal

When you see an opportunity, how do you assess it? If it offers you the chance to make a lot of money, is that a good enough reason to go for it? It all depends on how much you need or want the money and how much you would enjoy the negotiation and the outcome that it promises. The world is full of people who are in jobs they don't enjoy very much because they thought they would like to get the money on offer. In many cases, money simply isn't enough to guarantee fulfilment.

If you see an opportunity and you are not sure whether to go for it or not, play with the idea for a while. Imagine what it would be like if you had what it offered. What would it be like if you had it in a year's time? What would you say to someone who asked you why you got it? What benefits will it bring you? What are the penalties of getting the deal?

For a moment, try to separate the facts or figures from your emotional response. What you are most frightened of is not necessarily what will happen. Equally, what you desire is not necessarily the most likely outcome. Ask yourself if you feel it is worth risking the downside to attain your goals.

In family negotiations there is more at stake than time and money. Intangible assets such as love, loyalty and reputation are brought into play and negotiations frequently have an effect beyond the specific people involved. Inevitably, family feuds have repercussions for all the members of the family, not just those who may be disagreeing. Even simple deals around household tasks are more complicated with several children. If you come to an agreement with one child, the others will expect it to influence their agreements too.

EVALUATE AN OPPORTUNITY

To help to evaluate an opportunity, get all the details down on paper so that you can look at them.

- Draw a line down the middle of a piece of paper.
- On the left-hand side, write down the potential benefits of the deal.
- On the right-hand side, write down the possible losses or downside.
- Work out the possible combinations of outcomes and imagine how you would feel if they came true.
- Match up the risks and the rewards and decide how big the reward must be for you to be willing to take the risk.

Imagine, for example, that someone is offering you the chance of going into business with them. They have a small catering business, and in return for you bringing in some capital and your marketing expertise they are offering you half the business. On the left-hand side of the piece of paper you need to write down your estimate of your share of the profits per annum and your assessment of the value of the business in five years time if things go well.

On the right-hand side of the piece of paper goes the sum of money you are being asked to invest and a year's worth of your time. If the business goes bust in a year you could lose all that. Now it is down to you. Is the potential to make those profits worth running the risk of those losses? What would you have to do to maximize the profits and minimize the risks?

Opportunity cost

Every negotiation, and every deal, has an opportunity cost. The opportunity cost of a possibility is equivalent to whatever you have to forgo in order to take up that possibility. The opportunity costs of a negotiation increase with the time spent on it. If I spend ten days negotiating a deal to buy widgets from you, that is ten days I have not been able to spend sourcing an alternative supplier of widgets. If I decide to invest in your catering company, neither my time nor my money is available for any other projects.

It is not worth negotiating an offer if the improvement in the deal that you can hope to achieve is worth less to you than the opportunity to do something else with your time. It is also not worth spending time negotiating a low-value deal if it leaves you short of time to negotiate a more important, high-value deal. That is as true in relationships as in business.

So as you look at the opportunities to negotiate in your life, before you get too involved try to assess the opportunity cost. How long will it take? What will you have to give up if you take up this chance? How much do you value what it will bring you?

You will find it useful to bear in mind the opportunity costs when you get down to negotiations too. Negotiation also costs the other party time. Often a time-related offer is the clincher on a deal.

■ Win–win or win–lose

You want to achieve your goal, and the other party wants to achieve theirs. If you both succeed, the situation is known as 'win–win'.

If both parties feel they have won from the agreement it means that in the long term the relationship between the two is friendly and trusting. If you are negotiating with your boss, your employees, your partner or your neighbours, therefore, it is best to aim for a win–win situation. But note the words I slipped in – 'if both parties feel they have won'. Whether or not the other party gets what they started off wanting, it is your job as a negotiator to ensure that in the end they want the deal they get.

Just as importantly, if they get what they want, it helps to make them feel they really wanted it. The better they feel about the deal, the easier it will be to ensure compliance afterwards. That is why persuasion is such an important part of negotiation.

There is another style of negotiation known as 'win–lose'. In this the first party tries to win all the advantages and leaves the second with the raw end of the deal. Some negotiators even go so far as to rate the success of their deals not on what they win, but on the extent to which the other party loses. This style of negotiation does not build trust. If someone feels they have lost out on a deal they will be that much more difficult to do business with afterwards.

Furthermore, this fundamentally aggressive approach tends to produce the same effect in negotiation as it does in other fields: aggression breeds aggression. If you try to screw the other guy, sooner or later he will try to screw you. In other words, if you go for 'win–lose' you run a higher risk of ending up with 'lose–lose'.

This is not to say that an aggressive approach does not produce results. In some cultures it is the norm to bargain hard. But in almost all circumstances it is preferable to be assertive rather than aggressive. It is of course important to know how to deal with an opposite party who negotiates aggressively. All the tactics and attitudes in this book can be employed very effectively to resist an excessively aggressive negotiator.

Because negotiation is founded in attitude and character, someone's style of negotiation is a fairly accurate reflection of their character in the rest of their lives. Joe is one of the most financially successful, yet aggressive, negotiators I know. He has increased the turnover of his business by nearly 50 per cent each year for five years. He is a very hard negotiator who continually pushes down the prices he pays. If he does a deal and he doesn't like the outcome he tries to force the other party to renegotiate.

Joe's relentless and naked pursuit of profit does not make him many friends but it suits the marketplace in which he operates. His behaviour illustrates two points. First, his style of negotiation reflects his character. He is not a very relaxed person, nor is he the easiest person in the world to get on with. In getting the best deal out of people, he doesn't seem to get the best out of them in any other sense. Secondly, the more aggressively someone negotiates, the more work you will have to put in to ensure that the other party delivers what has been agreed.

■ Setting your goals

Successful negotiators know what they want. In general terms we all know what we want. We all want to be healthy, wealthy and happy. We would all like to get a bargain when we are buying and a wonderful price when we are selling. But successful negotiation entails being more specific than that. What exactly do you want?

Really successful negotiators really know what they want. Before you start negotiating, decide exactly what you want to achieve. Focusing your mind very clearly on your goal is vital to guide your strategy and to enhance your personal power.

Your goal provides the motivation and the orientation of your negotiation. It provides you with a clear idea of what you will and what you will not accept. Having a clear goal enhances your determination. That is transmitted to the other party by all your non-verbal behaviour. When your posture, your tone of voice, your timing and every part of your emotional communication is congruent with achieving your success, you are sending an immensely powerful message to the people you are dealing with.

A clear mental focus on your goal enhances your persistence. It helps you to keep going even when it is not clear to you how you will succeed. Sometimes in complicated or contentious negotiations considerable persistence is necessary. When you keep focused on the goal, eventually a path towards settlement will appear.

The focus on your goal also stops you becoming too attached to a particular means of getting there. If a proposal is going nowhere you can drop it. It is not uncommon for several unsatisfactory proposals to be negotiated lengthily before both parties realize they will not work. If you are focused on the goal, that doesn't matter. You can let those proposals go and work up another one. What matters is the final agreement, not how you got there.

In strategic terms, focusing on what you want helps to marshal your thoughts and keep your energies orientated in the right direction. Negotiations are conversations and just like conversations they can meander. Keeping your goals in mind helps you to make sure the meandering is towards what you want and not too much towards the other party's interests.

Settlement range

In a financial negotiation you should have two ingredients clear: your target price and your limit of what is acceptable. If you are buying, your target price will be low and your acceptable limit will be the most you are prepared to pay. If you are selling, you will have a high target and a minimum you are prepared to accept. The range between your high and your low price is known as your settlement range. Your goal is to agree on a price in that range as close to your target as possible.

In emotional situations goals may well be less clearly defined. Often the goal will be simply to achieve an agreement. The mutual recognition of agreement may be more important than the specific issue.

There are several ways to work out your targets and your acceptable limits. If you are negotiating a contract, for example, a useful question to ask yourself to find your minimum is: 'How much do I need to be paid in order not to feel ripped off?' If you are selling something, imagine someone taking it away from your house or office and imagine looking at a sum of money in your hand. How much money do you need in your hand to feel good about seeing that object leave your possession?

Don't be limited by your first thoughts, stretch your imagination a bit. Don't settle for what you initially think would be just wonderful. Are your talents or possessions only worth that little? Of course, if you start every deal thinking you are going to get the bargain of the century you might be disappointed. However, it is better to err on the side of ambition. If your goals are too low, you don't make the most of your potential.

If you cannot fix a clear goal in mind, think very carefully before you enter negotiations. If you don't know where you want to go, the chances are you will end up just where the other party wants you.

■ Prioritize your goals

In all but the simplest of deals, there are many different elements to the potential outcome. Imagine, for example, that you are organizing a fundraising run for charity and you are seeking sponsorship from a local business. You can offer them advertising and an association with good causes that will enhance their reputation. In return, you might be looking for a cash donation to your chosen charity, prizes for the fastest runners, transport for officials, help with stewarding, refreshments for runners, printing of programmes, publicity and so on.

Before you approach the decision-maker at your potential sponsors, you need to prioritize your goals. For example, you could decide that stewarding, printing, the top three prizes and a donation of no less than £X are your essential goals. Your important goals are to have help with publicity, as many prizes as possible and a larger donation if possible. Nice to have, but less important, would be transport for officials and free refreshments.

In most negotiations there will be a range of desirable outcomes and you may have several goals. Some things will be more important to you than others, so prioritize.

PRIORITIZING GOALS

- Jot down a list of all the possible benefits you could aim for in your negotiation.
- Divide them into three groups in descending order of importance:
  essential
  desirable
  nice to have

When we look at the process of trading proposals in Chapter 5, this list will help you to decide your strategy. It is also useful to make a note of your essential and desirable goals and keep it with you during negotiations. If the process is long or complicated, it is advisable to check your list before agreeing any important steps to ensure that you have not forgotten anything. It is often best to excuse yourself and go somewhere private to check your list. Some negotiators are good at reading writing upside-down and they, like you, will make use of any information that comes their way.

Gathering information: the context

Even in the simplest negotiation there are a minimum of three critical factors: two people and the context. If you have prepared yourself and you are fully aware of the context you have done two-thirds of the work before you even meet the other party.

Jim was interested in buying a house that was advertised for £425,000. At the time the housing market was in the doldrums. It had been falling for some time and, as ever, no one knew where it was going next. He made an offer of £412,000, which was rejected, so Jim offered £415,000. When that offer too was rejected he had a long talk with the estate agent and heard the following story. The vendor had originally put the house on the market a year before for £495,000. He had received an offer for £480,000 but rejected it as insufficient. That buyer went off and bought somewhere else. Eventually the vendor reduced his price to £480,000 and received an offer of £460,000, which he rejected. After all, he reasoned, he had already been offered £480,000. The second buyer refused to offer more and also bought else-where. The vendor took the house off the market. But he still needed to move so a few months later he put it back on the market, which had weakened in the meantime, for £450,000. He was offered £430,000 and rejected it. Again the buyer went away. Now the house had been reduced to £425,000. It was clear to Jim that the vendor was fixated on getting his asking price but was ignoring the context. By refusing lower offers he had consistently failed to sell the property for what the buyers in the market thought was a fair price. All the offers he had received earlier were higher than his current asking price.

Jim realized that all the previous bidders had done his work for him, so he raised his offer to £425,000 and the vendor accepted it.

For a year the vendor had ignored the context of the weakening housing market and stuck to his asking price. Jim acknowledged that the market was still weak, but in his judgement the valuation was now reasonable enough to pay the asking price. A few years later he sold the house for a million pounds.

Context is always significant in negotiation. If you know more about it than the other person you have a great advantage. In each deal different ele-ments of the context will have greater saliency, but you can never know for certain whether another element will suddenly become more important. Family dynamics, exchange rates, market sentiment, competition, politics, leg-islation, planning policy and the weather can and do impact on negotiations every day.

Your pre-negotiation inspection of the context is a bit like a pilot's pre-flight checks. He checks that his aircraft is fully fuelled and serviceable. He must find out the prevailing weather and the likelihood that it might change. If it is particularly severe he will choose not to fly.

■ EXPLORING THE CONTEXT

■ Take nothing for granted. Check that your information is up-to-date, that your assumptions are correct and that your beliefs are grounded in fact.

■ Imagine that you are looking at the context from an external point of view. What does the situation look like from the outside?

■ What would be your assessment of your own position if you imagined describing yourself from the outside?

■ Are there any third parties who have an interest in the topic of your negotiations? What will be their reactions to your proposals?

■ Are there any third parties who could radically affect the context by actions unrelated to your negotiations?

■ Is the context liable to change? If so, what could happen, and what, if any thing, could give you an indication that change was about to occur?

■ Gathering information: the other party

The more you know about the other party, the better. But first of all, check that you are dealing with the right person. Do they have the authority to make the decisions that you require? Do not waste time negotiating with someone who cannot deliver the agreement you want. If you are dealing with a large corporation, insist on getting an appointment with someone in a position to buy what you want to sell.

When you find out who you need to talk to, find out as much as you can about them. What are they like? If you are dealing with a business, find out about its range of products and services, its policies and plans. Ten minutes browsing a website is very valuable to get a sense of a company's character.

Is the other party prepared or ready to negotiate? If you are the first person to have seen the possibility of a deal you may have to convince them that it is worth their while to consider it before you can move on to making them an offer they will take seriously.

If you are dealing with a private individual or a sole trader, find out about their idiosyncrasies. What can you discover about their history, their interests and habits?

If you are dealing with an individual you have not met before, try to talk to someone who knows them or has done business with them before. Are they everything they appear? A flamboyant big spender is not necessarily wealthy. They might be running their lives on credit.

If you already know the other party, don't assume that your knowledge is adequate for negotiation purposes.

ASSESSING THE OTHER PARTY

- Imagine that you have to describe this person to a colleague or boss, and consider the key points you would mention. Write them down. Remember to stick to what's relevant to the negotiation.
- Why would the other party negotiate with you?
- What do they need? Why are they negotiating rather than buying what they want elsewhere or just taking it?
- What alternatives to negotiation does the other party have?
- What does the situation look like from their point of view? Put yourself in their shoes. What does it feel like?
- What pressures are they under? Do they have a timetable to work to or a deadline to meet? Do they need to sell quickly? If, for example, you are buying a house from someone who needs to move fast, then you have an extra bargaining point if you have finance in place and have nothing to sell. In these circumstances, you could make a lower offer than someone who still has a house to sell.

Understanding the other party

Successful negotiators spend nearly half their time thinking about the other person's point of view and needs. The better you understand the other party, the more easily you will be able to present your proposals in a form that appeals to them. Just as you will be negotiating to achieve your goals, the other party will be trying to achieve theirs. The more you understand their perspective, the better you will be able to deal with their proposals and even direct them to your advantage.

■ PREPARING RESPONSES

■ Imagine you had to promote the other party's interests. How would you do it?

■ Think up as many arguments as you can for why you should accept the deal they are offering. Write each of them down in note form.

■ Work through this list of arguments and find a way to rebut each of the points.

■ Think of what they are likely to offer you and describe it in terms of what it would cost them.

■ Now think of what you would like them to accept and describe it in terms as similar as possible to those in which you have described their offer.

■ Use these arguments and descriptions to respond when the other party makes their proposal.

■ Hidden agendas

What is the other party trying to achieve? Are they just humouring you? Why would they want to complete on this deal? If you can't see a reason, it doesn't mean there isn't one. It may just be that their agenda is quite different from yours. Someone might enter negotiations with you just to distract you from another opportunity that they hope to corner behind your back. They might even negotiate in order to stop an agreement being reached. If their interests are best served by delaying agreement they will continue to produce difficulties and arguments while all the time claiming that they hope to settle. Someone could negotiate with you just in order to sow dissent and mistrust between you and others.

Thomas is a financier in the City of London. He was trying to persuade an investment fund to buy into a new type of bond that was effectively a combination of insurance and shares. The bond would pay a dividend determined by the performance of the different elements. The fund managers were keen to invest, but as it was a new type of bond they were also cautious. They queried the allocation of profits on each of the different elements; in particular, how much was allocated to the dividend and how much to the management. Thomas fought long and hard over the distribution of the profit from one element, an allocation of reinsurance. In the end he managed to retain only one percentage point more than might have been expected.

Thomas told me the story of his deal and how happy he was to have reached it. I asked him if his long, hard fight had been worth it, given that he had only gained one percentage point on a small part of the overall deal.

'Absolutely!' he replied. 'I don't really care about that percentage at all. I was only fighting for it to persuade them there was going to be a profit there to divide. I very much doubt if there will be, but I had to build that element into the bond in order to get a slice of the bits I did want. Consequently I had to get the investment fund to buy it too.'

Be careful when you do business with someone like Thomas.

■ Cultural issues

As global capitalism has become more widespread, more and more business-men have learned to deal with what are know as 'western' values. However, it is both interesting and valuable to explore and appreciate other modes of business and sociability – doing business will be easier and you might just gain some negotiating advantage. If you are intending to work or trade in a foreign country, take the time to learn the local customs.

If you do not have the means to do so, and you don't speak the language, you should seriously consider engaging a local agent. An agent will know the local customs and should also have local connections, which are invaluable. The agent, of course, has a living to make and you will need to negotiate with him or her just as you negotiate with your suppliers or customers. If you do not have time to sound out an agent, and you do not know local customs, think twice about trying to do business in an unfamiliar territory.

Conforming to social customs in different cultures around the world will strengthen your rapport. Behaving impolitely through ignorance will make your business more difficult.

In Arab countries, for example, you should always accept tea or coffee if it is offered to show your appreciation of your host's hospitality. Personal relationships are all important and you should take time to build them. Learn to enjoy small talk and conversation and get to know your host, without asking intrusive questions. Rather than ask about family, talk about your travels, the weather, the country or exhibitions you have visited.

It is impolite to broach the subject of your negotiations as soon as you meet. Wait until your host mentions the topic and then you can begin to lay out your proposal. Even when the topic is mentioned, subtlety is valued and respected. Above all in the Arab world, patience is a virtue. There is a long and noble tradition of sheiks being available to petitioners of whatever status or background, and this is expressed by a policy of having a door open to visitors at all times. In such circumstances, if your own negotiations were interrupted by another party, it would be polite to wait and return to your business when you are invited to do so.

In America the opposite is true. You are expected to get down to business as soon as possible. Time is money and wasting someone's time is as impolite as wasting their money. Harvey is an agent who had a TV tie-in book to sell in the United States. He had a big star signed up who had agreed to commit himself not just to the project but to the publicity drive as well. Harvey contacted all the publishers who were potential bidders for the book with an email outlining the project and giving them 48 hours to respond with an indication of serious interest if they wished to proceed to the next stage of meeting the star and making a bid.

When the publishers came to his office, Harvey greeted them from behind a desk covered in their competition's brochures. Meetings were short, high energy and high pressure. Each publisher was given 24 hours to come up with their best offer.

Henry was selling the same TV tie-in book in Britain. He called potential buyers and told them what was on offer. He had a few preliminary meetings and then invited all who had expressed an interest to meet the star at the centre of the project. He made sure none of the publishers met each other on the way in or out, and he cleared his desk of all competitor material between each meeting. As he put it, 'I want to make them feel good about the whole thing. My approach is to say: Welcome to this wonderful opportunity. If you pay the price you can be part of something special.'

Both Harvey and Henry negotiated excellent deals for their client by working with the culture of their respective buyers. The Americans responded well to the time-pressured, highly competitive set-up, and the British responded to the warmer, gentler approach outlining a more collective project. Generally speaking in Britain a slightly slower and less intense style of negotiation is more successful than the swifter style favoured in the USA.

In Asia yet more politeness and subtlety is expected. To admit one has a problem, or that one has made a mistake, would be to lose face, and losing face is felt to be very shaming. Topics are best framed in positive terms, not as problems and never as threats. Face is so important that sometimes people will agree to deals that lose money in order to save face.

Preserving face means that in Asia people are extremely reluctant to say no, lest it appear they are ignorant or impolite. As a result they will say 'yes' even when, to an occidental mind, the answer should be 'no'. Therefore, if you need to get clear information, phrase your enquiry as an open question. Instead of 'Can you do X?', try asking a question such as 'If someone was thinking of doing X, where would you recommend they begin their enquiries?'

It would be wrong to think that the phenomenon of 'face' is confined to the East. In the West, face can also be very important, although it is often understood in terms of pride or self-image. A taxi driver once told me about the £40,000 Jaguar he owned. When he admired it in the showroom, he felt the salesman was looking down on him, as if he didn't have the money to buy such a car. The driver told me, 'I thought, I'll show him, and I bought it there and then.' He had a magnificent car, but his pride cost him a lot of money too.

The issue of face means that in Asia you approach negotiations in quite a different manner from one you would use with Europeans or Americans. In Europe or America negotiations are often started by all the parties setting out the problems to be resolved so that it is quite clear what the goals of the negotiation must be. In Asia it would not be helpful to talk about problems at all. Keeping your goal in mind, you would initiate a conversation in which you indirectly offer the other party the opportunity to mention the topic that you wish to resolve.

Tony runs the Far Eastern office of an international freight business. He has learned over the years that if he asks his local workers to sort something out, they will not come to him if they meet a problem, because to admit they have come across something they cannot deal with would be to lose face. Instead, they will simply stop working on it.

Tony has to use his negotiation skills to ensure that his employees do their jobs. He has to regularly check the progress of their work and offer the assistance or guidance they need without letting them lose face. He has become expert at casually mentioning what they need to hear.

Other local customs that have nothing to do with negotiating can be just as important. In southern, rural Spain, if you empty your glass of wine it means you would like some more, and your hosts will keep you company. My friendly enquiry about supplies from a local farmer ended up with both of us quite incapacitated. I kept thinking I would politely finish what was in my glass and he, just as politely, insisted on refilling it!

▓ Asking what-if questions

You've set your goals, you've reconnoitred the context, you've learned about the other party and something about their culture. So now you are ready to start negotiating. No, not quite. So far we have concentrated on what you want, and what you might need to do to ensure the other party is happy to help you. But before you are ready to talk to them, you must ask yourself, what if something goes wrong? In fact, what if everything goes wrong?

Imagine you are on holiday on a Greek island and you decide to buy a dilapidated house in the most enchanting situation. It has a beautiful view and charming proportions. It just needs the roof fixed, a bit of plastering and the plumbing renewed. You make an agreement with a local builder to do the work. He explains he will need the money up front to buy materials and pay his workers. The job will be done by the time you return in three months.

What if in three months' time he has had your money and the work is not done? Is it wise to agree to hand over all the money up front? It might be a better idea to set a number of interim stages and arrange payment when pictures are sent of the process and completion of each stage. It will, of course, cost a little more to arrange for a number of smaller payments, but if you hand over all the money straight away, you will have no more control over the work. It is better to retain some bargaining power until you are satisfied that you have got what you are paying for.

In the preparation stage, write a little list of all the things that could go wrong. If you hire a car, what happens if it breaks down? If you hire a driver, what happens if he doesn't turn up? If you form a partnership, what happens if your partner withdraws? What happens if you agree a profit share on sales to a third party and the third party drops out? If you buy a half-share in a boat, what happens if your co-owner sinks it? If you get married, what happens if your spouse decides to divorce you?

Asking 'what if' will help you to draw up a list of conditions for your agreement. If you are buying a piano, what if it is out of tune? You could agree to buy it subject to inspection by a qualified piano tuner. If you are replacing your fridge, what if the new one doesn't fit? Agree to buy it only when you have checked the measurements. Ask 'what if' before you start negotiating, and keep asking it throughout the process.

The other party might try to dissuade you and tell you that you are worrying about nothing. The correct response is to agree that may be so, but you would rather do a little worrying now that later proves unnecessary than find yourself in a situation where you have a lot to worry about and no way to remedy it.

▓ Best alternative

The other party doesn't have to accept your offer, and you don't have to accept theirs. In fact, you don't have to negotiate at all. You can always walk away. Before you start talking to the other party you need to be clear what is your best alternative to negotiating this agreement. Knowing the level at which you can walk away and still find a satisfactory alternative stops you from being persuaded to take a less than acceptable deal.

For example, you might be considering buying a new car. Your own car still works well and is worth about £5,000. You have an extra £5,000 pounds. You see a beautiful car advertised for £12,000. You get the price down to £11,000. What do you do next? Do you want to borrow another £1,000? Before you do, think what is your best alternative. It could well be to keep your current car, keep your money and wait for a better deal. Then your final offer to the vendor can be a powerful one. 'I don't have to buy this car,' you tell him, 'and this is all I have, so you can either sell it to me for £10,000 now or hope for a richer buyer later.'

The other party also has a best alternative. They could do a deal with someone other than you. If you are negotiating a pay rise, for example, work out how much it would cost your employers to replace you, and make sure that the rise you ask for costs them less than that. When you know your best alternative, you remain in a good position whatever the outcome of the negotiation. Either you get what you want at a price you are willling to pay, or you move on to a better alternative.

■ Time and place

When you know what you want and what you are prepared to offer for it, decide what is your preferred schedule for negotiation. The other party may have theirs, but, once again, decide what you want before simply conforming to other people's wishes. What style suits you – informal, businesslike, imposing or friendly? If you are free to choose the location, think about what sort of an atmosphere you want to create. Do you want to invite them to your own office or home? It has the advantage of being home territory, but it makes it more difficult to walk out of the negotiations and it may be difficult to persuade the other party to leave.

In family negotiations consider carefully whether a neutral environment would be helpful. If feelings are running high it can be a good idea to go out for a walk in the countryside where there is plenty of space for vigorous talk and exercise and the surroundings can help establish a sense of proportion. If you have a dog to take with you, so much the better.

■ Final check

Before you go to open your negotiation conversation, make a final check of what you have established so far. What are your goals? If the deal is financial, what is your settlement range? What are the potential variables of your offer?

What supports do you have for your argument? The more you have ready at this stage the easier it will be for you to move the other party towards a position you find acceptable.

Do you know enough about the context in which you are operating? Are there other forces at play about which you need to know? What do you know about the other party? Why are they negotiating with you? Find out, if you can, what their best alternative to negotiating with you might be.

To complete your check, imagine being a third party listening as you make your proposal to the other party. What information can you gather from that point of view? Now imagine once more seeing the situation from the other party's point of view. What does your offer sound like from there? Does this perspective give you any indication as to the best order in which to present your proposals?

Have you set up some variables that you can let the other party win? It is important to ask for more than you want so that you can let the opposition gain something and feel that they have beaten you down as you move them closer to what you want.

In the light of all these questions, do you think you need to revise your goals or restructure them? Do you need to break them down into stages? Decide if it would be worth your while to go ahead if you achieved only half your objectives. What conditions would make that acceptable? Make sure you are clear about your best alternative to negotiation and make a note of it.

When you have decided on your key goals and key supports, make a list of them. At the very least have a list of the key areas and concerns that you need to cover in your negotiation meeting, and take that list to the meeting. Do not put it face up on the table! Have your list in your pocket, and if you need to consult it do so in private.

It is possible that issues and proposals will come up in negotiation that you have not thought of. The more preparation you have done the easier it will be to assess and value those new proposals. The point of preparation is not to control the negotiation from start to finish, but rather to be able to keep your balance and keep moving towards your goals, whatever comes up.

Say what you want, not why

Chapter 4
Opening

❏ Getting attention and building rapport

❏ Saying what you want

❏ Setting up 'yes'

❏ Establishing a price

The time comes when you have to propose a deal. Of course, your negotiation process has started long before. You will have spent plenty of time in information-gathering and all your personal preparation will have readied you for the task. Personal preparation means you will be ready even when you have to negotiate without warning.

■ Pragmatism

Negotiation is thoroughly pragmatic. When someone approaches you with an offer, ask yourself: Why are they negotiating with me? What have I got that they want?

The motors of commerce are fear and greed. In other words, people deal because they see the opportunity for gain or they fear the possibility of loss. Someone proposing a deal believes you to have some capability or asset which they hope to obtain on favourable terms from you. The more you know about the specific details of what they want, the better. Whether the proposition is financial, social or emotional, the same principle applies. Ask yourself: What do they want from me?

In any given deal there will be a number of different pressures operating on each party. Some bear more on one party than another; some are universal. Your preparation should have revealed these. If you have not had time to prepare, there are some obvious candidates to check. For example, in business there is always some time pressure. A potential deal creates a certain amount of excitement, which creates an energy and a certain urgency. If the deal is not done in a reasonable amount of time, the energy dissipates and other possibilities arise to distract both parties.

Third parties can create pressure on negotiations. Sometimes there is a limited window of opportunity. A property deal, for example, may hang on the chance to get planning permission before local planning policy is changed.

Financial issues can also generate pressure. If a business has a number of employees, it needs a constant cash flow to pay for them. It has to do a certain amount of business to service its overheads. Private individuals, on the other hand, may have less of a need to deal. But someone with debts needs at the very least sufficient income to pay the interest and will experience some pressure to earn enough to pay them off. There are exceptions to this rule. If you owe the bank a thousand pounds they can make your life uncomfortable. But if you owe them five million pounds the power balance shifts towards you.

■ Official negotiations

If you have had a lot of warning about forthcoming negotiations, be suspicious. Whenever negotiations are officially signalled and set up a long time in advance, the chances are that most of the important work will already have been done before the formal sessions take place. In politics, for example, the real business is almost always done before, or occasionally after, the official meeting of the delegations.

Large companies or governments sometimes attempt to ensure a level playing field by putting business out to tender. The idea is that because each tender is examined anonymously all the parties bidding for the contract compete on an equal footing.

The actual effect of such procedures is simply to displace the negotiation. The real negotiation takes place beforehand between the potential bidders and the persons charged with drawing up the tender. Each bidder will try to influence the specification so as to ensure that it most closely coincides with what their own business has to offer, and if possible includes a requirement that the competition would be unable to deliver at a reasonable cost. If they do their job well, the contract is won before the tender is even announced.

■ Disclosure

What you disclose, and how much, will affect your bargaining position. As a general rule, you should only disclose information or facts that advance your cause, either directly or by building rapport. The most common mistake people make is to say too much. As power is to a great extent the perception of power, it follows that what people perceive can have a significant effect on your negotiations. If you walk into a house and your partner declares in rapturous tones that it is quite the most wonderful house in the world and that they have totally fallen in love with it, your capacity to persuade the vendor he needs to sweeten his offer is somewhat compromised. Similarly, if you are under extreme pressure to buy a house within the next fortnight it is not to your advantage to tell that to the vendor.

While it is not advisable to lie, it is very advisable to be careful about how much of the truth you reveal. It is often better not to disclose any pressures that are bearing on you and not to reveal your whole hand. However, whatever you do say, always base your response on facts that you know to be true. In this way your authenticity is maintained and you do not have to worry about maintaining any fictions. It is safer, practically, legally and morally, to tell the truth.

■ Get their attention

James was minding his own business at his office one day when his colleague leaped out of his chair shouting and waving a piece of paper.

'Yes, yes, yes!'

'What's going on, Frank?' asked James.

'I've got them,' replied Frank. 'Look.'

He showed James the letter. James read it. It was a polite letter rejecting Frank's offer.

'I don't get it,' said James. 'Basically they're telling you to get lost.'

'Yes,' said Frank, 'but now they're talking to me. Before they weren't even answering my letters.'

Frank caught their attention. Once the other party has entered into conversation with him, he can begin to work it round towards a deal. He is, you will deduce from this scene, persistent, optimistic, solution-focused and goal-orientated. That makes him an excellent negotiator.

It is often the case that at first only one person sees the possibility of a deal. If so, their first task is to catch the attention of the other party. In the retail world this is done with 'special offers' and 'summer promotions' and the like. In the commercial world it is done by what is known as a pitch.

In other contexts you just have to get a conversation going. If you want your neighbour to pay half the cost of replacing the fence between your two properties, your first job is to get him talking before you can persuade him of the benefits of replacing the fence.

▓ Rapport

Once you've caught their attention, you need to build rapport. Being in rapport means getting on well. The better you get on, the better the conversation flows, the easier it is to negotiate. In general people find it easier to get on with people with whom they have something in common. So the easiest way to build rapport is to find what you have in common and do more of it.

In a conversation, the easiest place to start is in the way you talk. You've probably noticed that if someone talks a lot more slowly than you, you don't feel you are on the same wavelength. Similarly, if they talk much faster you might find it difficult to connect. They will feel the same. It follows that if you bring the speed at which you are talking more in line with their speed, they will feel more at ease. If they use short, simple sentences, do the same. If, on the other hand, they have a tendency to express themselves in long sentences with a certain amount of polysyllabic verbiage, you could match them by utilizing your own capacity for verbosity and taking plenty of time, and indulging in lengthy and detailed descriptions in order to make your point.

Don't try too hard. It is counterproductive to change your own language use too much in order to try to match someone else. It is more helpful to use what you are comfortable with to move a little bit closer to their style and speed of speech.

You can match them at other levels too. For example, if they use a lot of concrete metaphors – they talk about building a deal, getting a grip on things, laying down foundations and so on – then you can do the same. Talk about nailing things down, measuring up, being hands on and solid as a rock. If their imagination is more visual they might use phrases like 'seeing eye to eye', 'a spectrum of opportunities', 'scanning the horizon' and 'full-colour descriptions'. In this case, if you use visual metaphors as well, they will feel more at home. Talk about 'an eye for detail', 'drawing up plans', 'getting a deal in your sights' and so on.

Once again, it is not necessary or advisable to try too hard at this. Just a slight move towards the other party's way of expressing things can have a very positive effect. And remember always to build on your own natural capacities. It is far better to move a little way towards them while staying in your own natural abilities than to try to imitate every element of their speech, and in so doing to lose touch with your own natural modes of self-expression.

If in doubt, speak a little less. After all, the more they speak the more information you can gather, and most people feel respected and appreciated when they are listened to.

■ Setting up 'yes'

Remember we defined negotiation as a conversation leading to agreement. If you set up a pattern of agreement early on, it increases the tendency to agree as the conversation progresses. An easy way to do this is to ask questions to which the answer will be affirmative.

When you walk into a shop in a beach resort, the assistant may ask you if you are there on holiday. She's not doing it because she's not sure why you are there, she is trying to start a conversation in which your first word will be 'yes'. If she succeeds, she will have increased her chances of a sale by two factors. First she has engaged you in conversation, and secondly she has got you to say yes.

Once we start agreeing we have a tendency to carry on. There are some people who don't like expressing themselves in the positive. If you ask them how they feel, they say, 'Not bad.' When they look round a house they itemize all the faults before mentioning the good points.

By listening alertly in your preparatory conversation you will soon recognize these people and their patterns of speech. They are just as susceptible to agreement as the rest of us, but they have a habit of expressing themselves negatively. In order to get on with them, it is helpful to do the same. If you want to say something positive, phrase it as a double negative. Rather than saying, 'That sounds interesting', use a phrase such as, 'I wouldn't say I'm not interested in your proposal'. If you want them to reject something, tell them it is exactly what they want. If you want them to be interested in something, be dismissive of it yourself.

When you start to match the patterns of expression and speech of other people you will find that you get a feeling for their moods as well. When you sense their moods you can match that too, and, as the conversation progresses, you can gradually build a mood of cooperation by adding mentions of the benefits of your proposal phrased in terms of their point of view.

■ Credibility

A psychotherapist was once interviewing a new client. The client complained that his previous therapist was thoroughly unprofessional and did not take any notes at all. The new therapist immediately picked up a pad of paper from her desk and wrote down solemnly, 'No note-taking'. Different people have different criteria by which they judge your soundness. Some people feel happy if they know about your qualifications, others want to know where you live. It is not unknown for a quick-thinking negotiator to take a photograph of someone else's impressive office block and email it to a supplier who requests details of their premises.

This is the same principle by which accommodation addresses are sited in prestigious parts of town and salesmen like to drive smart new cars. A certain degree of ostentation is reassuring to clients who admire displays of wealth. A bit too much can be counterproductive. An enduring and successful stock market tip is to sell when the company builds a smart new headquarters.

Ultimately, as a good negotiator, you know that the best foundation for your credibility is your own capabilities, values and integrity, and that is what you will be looking for in other people too. However, some people and some businesses require external validation of your competence. If you are good at what you do, that should not be difficult to obtain. If you are not good at what you do, you should be doing something else.

When you assess other people, do not put too much trust in their qualifications. All the certificates in the world will not make a person honest, and the ability to pass an exam is not the same as the ability to do a job. As you build your experience you will find that the best way to judge others is by their actions, and your own intuition.

■ Opening

In business jargon 'opening' refers to making the first offer. For example, if I am interested in your antique bookcase, I 'open' when I offer you £500. When you open, the issue of valuation is revealed. The big question is, what is the best price to open at? When you are selling, how high can you go? When you are buying, how low should you start? In many cases your preparation and information-gathering stages will already have given you the answer. If every other five-year-old saloon car of this type is advertised between six and nine thousand pounds, you know what your range is. Your estimation of its condition and the value of its extras will determine where you place it in that range.

Most of us learn from experience. If you look back on your deals and can see that you have been a bit timid, ask a little more and offer a little less next time. If your offers don't get taken seriously because the other party says you aren't offering enough, raise your offers. At the opening stage your first priority is to get taken seriously; the final price will be a result of the whole negotiation.

As a rule, outrageous bargains are rare. Of course, negotiators like to talk about their best deals, so we hear more about those than the merely reasonable ones. Don't be misled into thinking everyone around you managed to beat the market. By definition, everyone can't. The only people who make millions overnight are people who already have millions. The rest of us go slower.

If it looks as though you are about to get rich very quick be extra careful. Deals that look too good to be true usually are. Getting rich slowly is a more plausible route. And it is better to have a good deal that delivers than a fantastic deal that goes wrong. Of course, the more deals you do, the higher your chances of coming across a really good one.

■ Say what you want, not why

When you have decided on a price, don't be shy of saying it. If you were shy of mentioning money, your practice in the mirror will have cured you by now. Just name your price. Do not, at this stage, justify it. Whatever reasons you have for valuing the other party's goods or service at this price you can use later, if necessary, to defend your valuation against their attempts to undermine it. Offering your arguments at this stage wastes them. Used later, you will make them work for you, and repay all the effort you put into research and preparation.

If you are buying an item with detachable extras, be clear from the start what you expect to be included for your offer. Hi-fi systems require cables, cars have warranties, boats have trailers and hotels serve breakfast. Make clear what you are expecting for your money. Do not assume anyone else shares your expectations; spell them out.

■ A fair price

I have noticed that at the stage when money is finally mentioned, people who are not used to negotiating sometimes falter. They are worried that the other person may not be getting a 'fair' price. Typically, the people who do this are kind and nice, the sort who always put other people first. These qualities are admirable. However, they are best deployed after negotiation, not during it. If you do not get a fair price for your goods, you will have nothing spare afterwards to give to charity.

Negotiation is actually a very fair way to conduct your business because it makes each of us responsible for our own rewards. No one is forced to accept your offer, any more than you are forced to accept theirs. If I accept your price, it is my decision. If it is a good price, I have something to be pleased about. If I later feel I have paid too much, it is a lesson I will remember. Either way, I have a benefit, and I also have the item I purchased.

If for any reason you are shy or hesitant before opening, it is a great time to get in touch with your confidence by pressing your finger and thumb together and remembering that feeling of complete self-belief (see pages 52–3). You will be surprised how soon you find it easy to name your price.

If you are the potential purchaser, at some point the other party will name their price. Whatever they say, it is, of course, too much. You have a range of means to convey your dissent, from a little shake of the head to outright incredulity. You can be understanding in a kindly way of their naïve optimism while conveying with regret your more realistic valuation. You can be firmly dismissive or thoroughly amused. You can be businesslike, outraged or down-to-earth. You will evolve your own style, but remember to vary it from time to time. Different people respond better to different approaches, and flexibility is part of your strength as a negotiator.

■ Advertised prices

If you are negotiating for an item that has a price attached, such as a second-hand car or a house, the vendor has effectively opened with the asking price. In this case your opening response is ideally as far as possible beneath what they are expecting while at the same time being sufficiently plausible to persuade them that it is worth starting to negotiate with you.

Again, all your information-gathering pays off here. If the other party is under pressure to sell, you can open lower than you otherwise would. Every market has conventions – but in a seller's market the seller has more freedom to break those conventions and in a buyer's market the buyer can do so. It is usual, for example, in the housing market to make an offer, and perhaps to put a time limit on it, say, that it must be accepted or rejected within so many days.

When Jack was buying a house the market was sluggish and he had found out that the house was a repossession that had been on the market for some time. The bank that owned it wanted to sell but were very dilatory. Jack wanted a quick decision and the best possible price. He offered £90,000 and stipulated that after one week his offer reduced by £500 per week. After two weeks they accepted his offer. He pointed out that the offer was now £89,000. One week, and another £500 later, they got the point and accepted.

If you are selling a house or car you obviously want your advertised price to be as high as possible. Your advertisement should give some indication as to why it is worth so much, but you should keep back several supports for your price. As negotiation gets under way you can expect a purchaser to challenge your price and you should have available some means to defend it which they have not already discounted.

■ Challenging fixed prices

In order to challenge fixed prices you need nothing more than the realization that you can. The best way to embed that knowledge is to practise. Make a habit of questioning every price and always ask for a discount. As we saw earlier, sometimes just asking is all that is necessary to get what you want.

Have you noticed that if you ask for something to eat in a restaurant, they ask you what you want to drink with it? They don't ask you if you want a drink, they ask you what you want to drink. The question presumes you will take something, and very often people do. More sales, and more profit, to the restaurant.

You meet the same type of question when you go shopping. Whatever you take to the counter, when you offer to pay the assistant usually asks if you want anything else with that. That one question increases their sales every day, by indirectly suggesting that you might want something else, and by creating another opportunity for you to ask for it. They are not wasting their breath with those words – they say them because they prompt people to spend more.

If you have any qualms about asking for a discount, remember those questions. You are only beginning to redress the balance if you reply to their questions, which are designed to make you spend more money, with one of your own that could help you spend less.

Never give something for nothing

Chapter 5
Doing the deal

❏ All offers are conditional

❏ Trading variables

❏ Discover their core values

❏ Using your emotional intelligence

❏ The negotiator's toolbox

magine you are very rich. You live in an enormous mansion. You need a gardener. A poor man approaches you one day and offers to look after your garden for ten pounds a day.

'I'm sorry,' you tell him. 'I don't need to pay that much. I can get the job done at the moment for eight pounds a day.'

'Maybe so,' says the poor man, 'but how well is it done for such a price? When I tend a garden every weed is banished, every flower is cherished and the soil looks good enough to eat. Surely a palace like this deserves the very best service.'

'Of course I want the best service,' you reply. 'I don't pay for a job done badly.'

'Ah, but so many people do,' replies the poor man. 'Why don't you let me show you the quality of my work? Let me do the job for a week and you will see what a garden looks like when the job is done properly.'

'I will pay you nine pounds a day,' you reply, 'provided the job is done perfectly. If I find a patch of the garden untended, you get nothing.'

'Very well,' says the poor man, 'I will work in your garden under those conditions provided that when you see that my work is up to standard, you will give me the contract at the same rate for a year.'

'All right,' you agree, 'but only if I can revoke the contract if I decide the quality of your work has fallen.'

'Agreed!' he replies. The pair of you shake hands and the gardener starts work.

You've just negotiated a deal. You've solved a problem. You've got someone to look after your garden.

He has solved a problem too. He now has an income. So you have both benefited.

And that is the essence of negotiation: reaching an agreement to solve a problem. I'm using the word problem in the widest possible sense here. Your problem could be that you have a five-year-old car and you want a new one. To solve that problem you need to find someone who wants a five-year-old car and someone, possibly the same person, who has a new car and would like to sell it. Or you might want to go out for the evening and your problem is needing a babysitter for your four-year-old child.

You might have a more complex problem, such as wanting your neighbour to support a planning application, or needing to win more customers for your business.

Every negotiation is unique. Each one solves a particular problem. But negotiation can do more than solve a problem: it can actually increase the benefits that accrue to all parties.

Let's look at your deal with the gardener again. What benefits have you got from this negotiation that you might not otherwise have got? First, you have a risk-free trial. If the garden is not tended to your satisfaction you don't have to pay anything. A corollary is that your gardener has the incentive to do a good job rather than simply going through the motions. Secondly, you've been offered a guarantee of quality and an effective sanction if he doesn't deliver: you can sack him. Thirdly, you are dealing with the principal. The gardener has negotiated his own deal and is delivering it himself. He has responsibility both for the deal and the delivery. By comparison, if you dealt with an agency there would be more potential for argument and avoidance of responsibility in the event of declining standards. You would have to rely on the agency exerting pressure on the gardener to improve. Fourthly, you have a contract for a year. Provided he keeps up his standards you won't need to spend time looking for another gardener for at least twelve months. Of course, all this comes at a cost – a pound a day more than another gardener might cost. But you have decided it is worth it.

What about the gardener? What benefits has he got? First, he's got some work. Secondly, he has got a good rate, a pound a day more than the competition. Thirdly, he has got steady employment – a contract lasting a year. Of course, it has cost him something too. He has taken the risk of doing a week's work and not getting paid if it is not deemed satisfactory. You have the right to refuse payment if you find a single weed in the garden. He has effectively agreed that your judgement as to the quality of his work will determine whether he gets the job, and whether he continues to keep it. These could be tough conditions, but he has decided they are worth accepting because he gets a premium rate of pay.

Of course, both you and the gardener could have said no. You could have found someone else to do the job, and he could have offered his services to someone else doing something else. So you both chose, of your own free will, to agree the deal, and the deal entails both of you complying with its terms. You have just agreed that what you give him is of equal worth to what he agrees to provide for you. In that sense your negotiation has achieved a certain equality. In spite of your wealth and his poverty, your mutual obligation puts you on an equal footing in the context of this deal.

Both parties, you and the gardener, have done well out of the deal. And you've both ended up with more than a simple exchange of labour for money. You get your garden kept in good shape, and a guarantee and continuity of delivery. He gets a good rate and continuity of employment. Negotiation, in other words, has allowed you both to get a better deal.

▦ All offers are conditional

In the story above, you and the gardener were swapping proposals. He offered a service for ten pounds. You rejected it. He tried again, claiming he would demonstrate his service was worth ten pounds. You rejected it again, but offered him nine pounds only if you judged it an excellent piece of work. If not, he would get nothing. He accepted your offer but only if you agreed to give him a year's contract if you deemed the quality acceptable. You agreed to that only if you had the right to cancel if the quality declined.

The absolutely essential element is the phrase *'only if'*. Every time either of you offered to accept any part of what the other proposed you made it conditional on them accepting something beneficial to yourself.

If you think of a negotiation as a journey towards agreement, the steps of the journey are conditional offers. Each time you offer something more to the other party you make it conditional on them offering more to you. This reciprocal exchange of conditions is what creates the deal. Without reciprocity, there is no negotiation, although there may be a deal, albeit a bad one.

Negotiation is the process of exchanging conditional offers, and *every move towards the other party's requests is conditional on them moving towards yours.* There are lots of other useful and important elements of negotiation, but this is more than useful, it is vital. *'Only if'* is what keeps a negotiation creating alternative options until both parties are satisfied.

'*Only if*' is what stops you being bullied. It stops you giving things away for free, and it pulls the other party either towards accepting your offer or towards coming up with an alternative.

■ Variables

The 'only ifs' that you exchange in negotiation are called variables. Anything that can vary the overall shape and value of a deal is a variable. All the different elements of a deal are potential variables. Price, payment schedule, delivery, quantity, quality, content, accessories, guarantees, servicing, colour, options, installation, training, range, upgrades, finish, fitting and so on are all variables.

Trading variables allows you to customize the proposal so that both parties get more of what they want. A variable is anything that makes a material difference to the deal. Some variables are more valuable to one person than another. You will get a good deal when you find a variable that costs little to you but is highly valued by the other party.

■ USING VARIABLES

- ■ Never dismiss any element of a deal as trivial or unimportant. It might be a variable that is highly significant to the other party.
- ■ As the conversation goes back and forth you want to make each of your variables count. So offer to negotiate only one variable at a time.
- ■ On the other hand, when the other party is making points or offering concessions, it is to your advantage to invite them to offer more. If they are attacking your price, listen to what they say and then respond, 'I have made a note of your points. Do you have any other concerns?'

The primary purpose of using variables is to rearrange the deal so that what suits you becomes more acceptable to them. Only if that doesn't elicit agreement should you consider reducing your benefits or increasing theirs. In other words, repackage, don't concede. For example, if the other party won't raise the sum of money they offer, reduce the overall value of the package they are getting for their money. If they are selling an item for a high price, ask for more extras to make it worth that much to you. If you are negotiating a fee and they want to reduce the guaranteed basic, your counter offer would be to increase the percentage on the performance-related element.

You can use and create variables to repackage your proposal in countless different ways.

Never give owt for nowt

Perhaps the single most important principle of negotiation is *never give something for nothing*. In Yorkshire they say, 'Never give owt for nowt.' If you alter a variable for the benefit of the other party, you should always do so only on the condition that there is another alteration that benefits yourself. By attaching conditions to every alteration you make, you ensure that the negotiation moves towards rewarding you at the same time as rewarding the other party. That is what the words 'only if' were doing in your hypothetical negotiation with the gardener. Every true negotiation is conducted on this principle. It ensures that you always retain control of your commitments and that you are always exerting pressure on the negotiations to lead towards your goals.

If you are facing a negotiator who insists that they need more from you than you have offered, and you cannot find a benefit to ask for in return, give them the problem. Ask them to find something else to your benefit that would make their offer more palatable.

Finally, stick to the principle of never giving something for nothing right to the end of negotiations, so that when you are close enough to a deal that you consider satisfactory you remember to offer to meet their price *only* if they agree right now.

■ MAKE EVERY OFFER CONDITIONAL

- ■ Never give owt for nowt.
- ■ If you can't find a variable that will recompense you for what the other party wants, ask them to find one.
- ■ If you are happy with what is offered, make your agreement conditional on the other party settling immediately.

Money

Money is perhaps the most obvious variable. The simplest way to improve a proposal is to offer more money. However, a good negotiator always makes that her very last resort. The purposes of businesses are far broader than simply making money, but unless you are cautious with your expenditure you risk ceasing to be in business at all if times get hard. As a general rule, when selling, explore all the other available variables before considering a reduction in your asking price. If the other party holds out for a lower price, attach any offer you make of a lower price to a variable that reduces the cost to you.

If you find that you do have to change your price more than once, ensure that the reductions or increments become smaller each time. Not only does this control your costs, it also increases the pressure to accept on the other party by giving the impression of getting closer and closer to a limit.

Intangible variables

Luke has a very successful, up-market interior design company. He knows that a fair number of his clients like to challenge his prices, not because they can't afford it, but because they don't like thinking they might be being ripped off.

On one occasion he was doing a large piece of work for a foreign couple on their London house. Both the husband and the wife were keen to avoid being seen as rich foreigners who could be charged inflated prices with impunity, and throughout the design process they negotiated skilfully. When it came to signing off the agreement so that work could start, the husband challenged his prices again.

'Surely,' said the husband, 'you have clients here in London who do not pay these prices.'

'Sir,' replied Luke, 'Buckingham Palace pays these prices.'

The contract was signed there and then. Both Luke and his client won something from their negotiation. Luke kept the business and protected his margin, and his client was reassured that he was not being taken to the cleaners.

Luke also gave his client a very valuable intangible benefit: the satisfaction of knowing that he shared a designer with a very prestigious customer. Intangible benefits such as this are worth so much to some people that they are willing to pay very high prices to get them.

■ Discover their core values

Imagine you are trying to persuade your neighbour's teenager to baby-sit for you. You might be reluctant to pay more than the going rate because she will then be more likely to expect the same rate in the future. If you keep talking and ask her what she likes about visiting other people's houses she might let you know that her own mum is a lousy cook and she likes other people's home cooking. So she likes money, but she likes good food as well. Then you know that maybe keeping a slice of your home-made pie back for her might be the clincher you need.

Babysitter or president of a multinational, the same principle applies. Find out what their core values are, and then find out the most convenient way to match them. Ask plenty of questions about what sort of benefits the other party is looking for. Use open questions that invite them to give detail rather than closed questions that can be answered with a simple yes or no. All the time you are looking for the criteria by which they judge quality and acceptability. The more you know about what they want, the more effectively you can use your variables to reshape your offer.

If the conversation does not reveal what those core values are, a series of questions of the form, 'And what will that give you?' can help to elicit them.

For example, imagine you are setting up a business with a partner. You need an office. Your partner wants it in the suburbs; you want it in the centre of town. You need to negotiate.

You ask why your partner wants the office in the suburbs and he replies that it is cheaper than the middle of town and easier for him to get to. The key to understanding this is to avoid assuming you know what that means to him. You must find out in very specific terms why cheapness is a benefit to him. Perhaps he will tell you that it makes him feel safer to limit expenditure and liabilities when the business is just starting up. Similarly, what, for him, is the benefit of it being easier to get to? Maybe for him it means that he can sleep in later in the morning.

Now, although these questions seem pretty dumb and the answers obvious, in the case of both of them it is possible to find other ways to meet those core values. You could have a smaller office in the middle of town with a shorter lease, and thus limit your exposure. You could arrange with your partner that he arrives at work later in the morning and then works on a little longer in the evening.

Of course, choosing an office involves far more factors than just these, but each of them can be tackled in the same way. Find out what is the value to your partner behind each of his preferences, and explore how many other ways you can satisfy those values.

You can also do the same thing yourself. He can ask you why you want to be in the centre of town. Maybe it is closer to your home, and easier for you to get to. Maybe you want the prestige of a central address. He can ask further questions to discover why ease of access is important to you. Maybe you don't like driving. Perhaps, therefore, he needs to suggest somewhere next to a convenient railway station. Similarly, he can suggest other ways that you can increase the prestige of your business, perhaps with expensive stationery or an impressive website.

■ A waste of time?

Isn't all this negotiating a waste of time, though? If you think you know where you are going to end up, isn't it just a charade going through all this business of trading variables and arguing? Why don't you just name your bottom line and agree it?

The first and most important reason why you cannot short-circuit the negotiation process is that the other party may not agree to do so. You may say that your offer is your bottom price, but they may treat your statement as a negotiating strategy. It is the first price you name so they attack it, and they won't feel ready to settle until they have got a real bargain.

Secondly, the negotiation process builds perceived value. If I have struggled hard to raise my salary by £2,000 per year I will value that increase more highly than if I was given it without having to make any effort.

Similarly, if I am selling my car to you we will both be happier if we have negotiated. Imagine that I have advertised my car for £12,250. If you start by offering £10,500 and I get you up to £11,500 I will feel good about the 'extra' thousand pounds I have extracted from you. Equally, as you have beaten me down from £12,250 to £11,500, you can feel good about the £750 you have 'saved'. Both of us have the experience that our efforts have been rewarded.

Thirdly, the process of negotiating builds commitment to the deal. We all have a tendency to value more highly whatever costs us effort to obtain. If negotiation takes time and effort it makes us value the outcome. Furthermore, both parties are responsible for the offers they made and hence are committed to them more personally than if they simply accepted a standard or fixed-price deal. Increased commitment means people are more likely to stick to their word and more likely to try hard to deliver, even if problems arise. Finally, but by no means least, negotiation increases the chance that both parties will find a better deal than was originally envisaged. If by challenging your proposal I prompt you to enhance your offer, I get more for my money. You may offer something extra that you did not initially realize would appeal to me. The same is true of what I offer in exchange.

For example, you might discover during our conversations that I am selling my car because I am moving to the United States. If you have a plentiful supply of dollars you could make your low offer more acceptable by volunteering to pay in US dollars. If I save more by not having to pay to convert my pounds to dollars than I concede to you for paying in dollars, I will accept. By negotiating we both get a better deal.

■ THE NEGOTIATOR'S TOOLBOX

As a negotiation unfolds, the other party will show more of what they are looking for and both of you will have opportunities to vary your offers, to expound the benefits of your own proposals and to move towards agreement. All the suggestions that follow are different ways you can do this. It is neither necessary nor possible to propose a specific order in which they should be used. It is rather like learning different tennis shots, such as the lob, the smash and the drive. Good players have them all at their disposal but how and when they use them depends on the opportunities they see and what the other player does. It is the same in negotiation.

All the techniques, strategies, ideas and stories that follow arise from approaching negotiation with the resourceful attitude that we described in Chapter 2. Use them wherever you wish. They are all tried, tested and successful.

This is not an exhaustive list. Human ingenuity is boundless and from these basic attitudes and principles an endless variety of approaches can be created. Do not feel limited to the ideas mentioned here. There are many more and many variations. Given the huge range of situations in which you can negotiate, it would be impossible to produce an exhaustive list. You can adapt these ideas or use them for inspiration to create your own. As you embed the attitudes of a successful negotiator, these techniques and others like them will come to you naturally.

▥ Intuition

How do you choose what to do? After a while experience will guide you. Often the other party's proposal will suggest a number of responses to you, and you can also use your intuition. Intuition is an excellent guide. Research into very healthy families conducted in the 1970s by J. Lewis and others revealed a strong link between psychological health and the use of intuition.[6] Wiseman's research into lucky people cited earlier (see page 35) showed a cor-relation between luckiness and paying attention to intuition and hunches. He reports several stories of good deals achieved and bad deals avoided by people who trusted their gut instincts.

Your intuition is the intelligence of your emotions. It is a gestalt response to all the non-verbal signals you are picking up from someone. It is your response to how congruent they are and the signals they can't control, which indicate their true intentions.

If you feel you don't trust someone, respect that feeling. It may not mean that you can't do business with them, but it does mean that you should double-check everything and take nothing for granted.

▥ Persuasion

In the conversation of negotiation, each party takes it in turn to speak. It is not necessary to amend your offer each time you speak. Sometimes, instead of changing your offer, you can use your turn to mention a reason why your offer is a good one. In other words, rather than modify your offer, you support it. You persuade the other party to appreciate better what you offered in the first place.

Perhaps the most obvious form of persuasion is to spell out the benefits of your proposal to the other party. This may sound simple but it is not to be forgotten. You cannot afford to assume that they have realized all the potential benefits. When you itemize them, the chances are you will mention something they had not thought of.

As you mention each item their response will indicate to you which items are more important to them, and hence which avenues and variables will be more rewarding to pursue.

There are a number of persuasive arguments that can be applied in some form to a great many offers.[7] One of the most common of such arguments is to claim that what you have is scarce. This is one of very few models in this colour, the last one in stock, the first in the country, the only one with air conditioning and so on. There is a solid body of research that has shown that we have an automated response to scarcity. If something is scarce, we have a tendency to desire it more than if it was in abundance. This is why limited editions are a favoured ploy of retailers.

Even more compelling than something scarce is something that is getting more scarce even as you watch. As the opportunity for purchase shrinks, the pressure to purchase increases.

Another common type of argument is known as social proof. This takes the form: 'Everyone else is doing it, buying it or saying it so it must be a good thing'. As we all know, this is far from logical, and certainly it is not always true. However, it is a semi-automatic pattern of human behaviour to believe that if other people are doing something, there must be a good reason for doing it. This is the reason that the populace in Hans Christian Andersen's story of the emperor's new clothes clapped and cheered at the beauty of the emperor's tailoring. The hero of the tale is the small boy who believes his own eyes and says, 'But the emperor is naked.' If you have to choose between believing what everyone else believes or believing in yourself, trust yourself.

Whenever people have paid a certain price, they have helped to establish that price. The advantage from the vendor's point of view is that the rationale for the price is out of his hands. It is simply the going rate and by implication he, and you, have to abide by it. To challenge this gambit one needs to establish that the vendor does have authority to amend the price, and that what is being sold is in some way, however small, different from the standard item.

Another common way to support a price claim is by comparative pricing. If I am selling my motorcycle for £5,000 I will mention that its performance is almost identical to that of another bike which costs £9,000. In two ways I make my bike appear good value. First, it offers the same performance for less cost. Secondly, by mentioning a price higher than £5,000, I am placing my price in the middle of a spectrum rather than simply at the top of the range you might have been considering.

Of course, it is a truism that whatever I am selling is cheaper than something else. The point of mentioning more expensive bikes that have something in common with my motorcycle is that they become part of the context that makes my asking price look more reasonable.

▨ Reframing

The essence of these and many other powerful arguments is reframing. Every judgement about a proposal is made in relation to a frame of reference. In the context of grocery shopping a difference of ten pounds is significant – in the context of buying a car it is not. The difference is in the frame. All discussions have an implicit frame around them, just like the frame around a picture. If I move the frame, expand it or contract it, I change the distribution of emphasis on the elements within it.

Salesmen who are trying to persuade you to take out a loan continually frame the cost in terms of monthly payments: 'You can surely afford fifty pounds a month.' They don't draw attention to the overall cost of the loan, including interest repayments over five years.

▨ Take it or leave it

Imagine that next door to your house is another large house with a big garden, which belongs to your neighbour, Bob. Bob, too, decides that he wants to employ someone to look after his garden.

A man called Charlie approaches him and offers to do the job for ten pounds a day.

'No chance,' says Bob. 'I can get the job done for eight pounds. Take it or leave it.'

Whatever Charlie says, Bob never changes his reply.

'I'll pay eight pounds a day. That's all, take it or leave it.'

What should Charlie do?

If Charlie doesn't take the job, both he and Bob still have a problem. Charlie would not have the income and Bob would still be without a gardener.

If he does take it, Bob would get his garden looked after, but Charlie would not have a clear incentive to do a first-class job. In fact, as Bob had been tough on him financially, the only way Charlie could get more benefit out of him would be by getting away with doing less work for his money. So, if anything, he would have an incentive to cut corners and do a bad job. Bob therefore will have to put more effort into supervising him to make sure he gets value for money. Bob saves himself a pound a day, but at the cost of extra time spent checking Charlie's work.

There is also a more subtle cost. By saying take it or leave it, Bob is treating Charlie not as an individual but just as another, interchangeable labourer. He is saying, 'I can get someone else to do this job for eight pounds. Who does it is of no interest to me.'

As a result the relationship between Bob and Charlie is not based on each respecting the individual position and commitment of the other. That in turn means that both parties will have little emotional commitment to the agreement. Whereas negotiation creates respect, fixed-price deals turn labour into a commodity.

You would not be entirely mistaken if this 'take it or leave it' attitude sounded to you uncomfortably like today's mass employment market. As we shall see later, negotiation skills are vital if you want to get yourself a better deal than an off-the-shelf job.

And what about Charlie? If he accepts Bob's 'take it or leave it' offer he hasn't negotiated. He didn't say, *'Only if ...'* He has a job, but he has no reason to have an emotional commitment to it, because there is nothing personal about the deal. There is nothing special to give him a sense of pride in getting the job, nothing to increase his respect for himself, or for Bob, and there is no incentive to do it brilliantly. It's just a job. 'Take it or leave it' without negotiation delivers much less than the negotiation, for both parties.

Of course, 'take it or leave it' does have some advantages for Bob. He is not going to waste any time negotiating and, as long as there are plenty of people looking for work, sooner or later someone is likely to take it. Bob may have decided that gardening is a straightforward job and performance is not going to be vastly improved by building more commitment into the deal. If someone does it well, they keep the job; if they don't, he'll sack them.

Persistence

But we haven't answered the question: what should Charlie do?

There are many possibilities. Just because Bob said, 'Take it or leave it,' Charlie is not forced to stop trying to negotiate. He cannot make Bob negotiate, but Bob can't stop him trying. Charlie's best bet is to start looking around for other work but until he finds something else whenever he sees Bob, or passes his house, he can have another go. He could, for example, come back with a conditional acceptance such as, 'I'll take it *if* you pay me one day's holiday pay per month.' Or he could ask Bob what other jobs he needs doing around the house to see if there is another point of entry. Each time Charlie tries to negotiate he is spending his own time doing so, but as long as he has no work he has plenty of time.

However, Charlie would also be sensible to spend some time researching other potential jobs, and he could use the information he gains in his further attempts to get Bob to negotiate with him. He could, for example, tell him of other similar jobs advertised at nine or ten pounds a day. In terms of his relationship with Bob, Charlie has almost nothing to lose. He can, in fact, use him to practise different engagement techniques on. Looked at like that, Bob is a wonderful opportunity for Charlie.

To sum up, Charlie should not take no for an answer, but he would do best to spend time finding some more people other than Bob who might say yes. Charlie should practise persistence, but he doesn't have to practise all his persistence on one person.

■ Creating variables

In your preparation you will have identified as many variables as you can. Then the other party's proposals will suggest some more. Sometimes, however, you may need to go a bit further and create new variables.

A young manager in an architectural firm was told to purchase a new plotter, an expensive device required to output plans. He was told that the most he had to spend was £20,000. He consulted the partners who would be using the machine and was told which one they wanted. He rang the suppliers. The machine they wanted cost just over £23,000. They were not willing to offer a discount. The machines were popular and there was no need for them to drop their price.

The young manager, wisely, went to consult the wily old head of purchasing. He heard the story and then rang the supplier.

The head of purchasing talked at length to the supplier about plotters and how much they cost, and manoeuvred the conversation so that the supplier agreed with him that if there were an ex-demonstration model, it would be sold at a discount.

Unfortunately, said the supplier, there were no ex-demonstration models.

Well, that was a shame. They talked some more, and the purchasing manager requested some more information about the plotter. He asked several questions, and said he really was very interested in this model, and asked if they could arrange to demonstrate it for him.

The supplier agreed. A demonstration could be arranged, and a date was set for the plotter to be brought to the office to be shown to the key users.

'Well,' said the purchasing manager, 'after the demonstration you would then have an ex-demonstration model, would you not? And it would, as we discussed earlier, be sold at a discount.'

The supplier agreed that would indeed be the case.

'Well,' said the purchasing manager, 'we have arranged a demonstration and that will of course be something of an expense of time and effort for your salespeople. Perhaps, if you can confirm the ex-demonstration price of £20,000, I could place the order right now and that will save you the expense of setting up the demonstration.'

And so the practice got its plotter for £20,000.

■ Silence

A simple and yet particularly effective technique in negotiation arises from its conversational structure of taking turns to speak. The cultural programming to do this is so strong that if one person does not speak the other one experiences a powerful pressure to fill the silence. In negotiation the pressure is reinforced because your silence implies that whatever they have said is not good enough to merit a substantive response.

When you are made an offer that's not good enough, and you have nothing to say, say nothing. Let the pressure build on the other party.

One of the reasons we talk to each other so much is because silence can be very intense indeed. A minute's silence can convey an enormous amount of emotional expression. Just sit it out.

USING SILENCE

- ■ When the other party's proposals are not realistic or if they are failing to take your suggestions seriously, respond to a question with silence. Fire your own confidence anchor, and wait for them to make an alternative proposal.
- ■ If you don't know what to say, try saying nothing.
- ■ If you are looking into someone else's eyes and you start to find it too intense to bear, focus on a point just at the bridge of their nose. You don't feel the pressure any more, but they still experience you as looking them in the eye.

■ Power

You don't always get to choose the situations in which you find yourself, but your way of being as a negotiator can help you out even in the most unpromising circumstances.

Through no fault of his own, Jim was being interviewed by a tax inspector. He had been asked to empty his pockets and it was explained to him that the Inland Revenue had the power to arrest him and seize all his assets. The Inland Revenue are able to make assessments and impose penalties on the basis of their own estimates. They can be extremely hard to challenge without years of documentation, which Jim knew he had not got. Jim felt understandably anxious.

'Have you ever had an offshore bank account?' asked the inspector.

'I had one in Jersey until a few years ago,' replied Jim truthfully.

'Oh really,' said the tax inspector, 'and why did you have that?'

'My dad told me to have it.'

'Oh did he?' said the inspector. 'And does your father have an account in Jersey too?'

'Yes,' replied Jim, 'he's had one there for about fifty years.'

'I think we may pay your father a little visit,' said the inspector.

'I think he'll tell you to get stuffed,' said Jim.

'I don't think so,' said the inspector.

'I think he will,' replied Jim.

'Now look here,' said the inspector, 'if anyone is going to do any "stuffing" round here it will be me.'

'I doubt it,' said Jim.

'And why exactly do you think your father can afford to tell Her Majesty's tax inspectors to "get stuffed"?' asked the inspector icily.

'Well, firstly, my father is a Jersey resident and you have no jurisdiction there. And secondly he's lived there since 1950 when he was invalided out of the armed forces having been injured defending your liberty,' said Jim. 'Now look. I don't like this. I don't want to be here and I want this sorted as soon as possible, but there is no need for you to jump to unwarranted conclusions about me or my father. If you ask honest questions, I'll give you honest answers.'

The inspector apologized and continued his enquiry in a more reasonable manner.

So who has the power in this relationship? The tax inspector has the legal power to seize anything he wants and the onus is on the citizen to prove that he does not owe any tax. However, in this situation, by arrogantly attempting to display his power, the tax inspector handed Jim the opportunity to undermine his position. Because the taxman had to continue a conversation with Jim in order to further his investigation, he was constrained to a certain degree by conversational conventions and Jim's intervention forced him to be both more respectful and more polite. No one is ever totally in control of a situation, not even the taxman. Without the approval of public opinion he cannot collect the taxes, as the British government found when it tried to impose a poll tax on its citizens. By being overbearing in his conversation he lost face and hence some of his power.

Threats are very, very rarely the best option in negotiation. If you have a good enough reason to use them, only actually do so if you are totally committed to carrying them out. A threat made but not followed through will seriously weaken your position.

Similarly, do not claim that something is not negotiable and then introduce it as a variable later on. Inconsistency like that reduces your negotiating strength and it also weakens trust. Far better, if you can't think of anything to say, is to say nothing.

Remember, the greater part of power is the perception of power. In any negotiation, whatever the circumstances, you always have some power as long as the negotiations are continuing, because the other party is still talking to you.

■ Use your information

Whatever your situation, your awareness and solution focus will help you see opportunities to improve your position. I was renting a property, and by the time the short-hold agreement was due for renewal my girlfriend at the time had moved out. The rent was quite a lot of money for one person to pay, but I had become used to the place and very much enjoyed living there.

Since I had moved in the landlord had moved abroad and had appointed agents to manage the flat. I realized that if I moved out the landlord would face significant costs. In that area agents typically charge one month's rent for finding a tenant. Furthermore, he would also face the probability of a void period in the property before he could get another person in. During that time no one would be paying him rent. I estimated it would cost him at least a thousand pounds to get a new tenant. So I divided a thousand by twelve – just over eighty – and realized that I should be able to negotiate a reduction of almost eighty pounds per month just for not moving out. And that's what I did.

■ Hard cash

For some people the sight of hard cash is very compelling. In his retirement Bill has taken to restoring antiques. He prowls the markets of France buying up old furniture. He always gets his stock at rock-bottom prices. How? He not only pays cash, he shows it to people. He always has several thousand Euros in cash in his back pocket. If he sees something he likes he pulls out his wedge and offers to buy for cash. *'Tout de suite! Immediatement!'* he exclaims, and waves his cash under the vendor's nose. His style and his enthusiasm to do the deal right now add to the persuasion of the cash. He always picks up bargains.

Even in the more sedate environment of the high street, cash can make a difference. Credit card companies charge retailers a fee of up to 4 per cent, so you should be able to negotiate a discount of 2 or 3 per cent for cash. Not only does the shop save the fee, but you are also offering a cash-flow benefit as they get their money straight away.

■ Play your losers first

If you know that there is something about the ultimate deal that you cannot avoid and that the other party will not like, it can be a good move to get it out in the open very early on. If the bad stuff is mentioned early on and they have accepted it, from then on things can get better.

Alternatively, it is possible to build up a great deal of agreement and then drop your bombshell at the last minute when there is so much momentum to get the deal to work that they are likely to accept it anyway. The disadvantage with this last-minute tactic is that it destroys a lot of goodwill and can make completion and compliance problematic. It also undermines trust because the other party can rightly complain that you concealed the bad news from them all during negotiations. It can even be a deal-breaker, and if it is it also will create bad feeling. If the problem is mentioned early on, even if they refuse to negotiate any further they have no grounds for resentment because you have been honest.

Therefore, unless there are compelling reasons for withholding it, mention a problem early on. It demonstrates honesty and realism and means that thereafter you move towards agreement rather than towards the problem.

■ Establish reciprocity

Humans have a natural tendency to reciprocate. If you buy someone a drink, they are likely to offer to buy you one back. The effect of reciprocity in negotiation is that if one party makes a concession, they expect the other one to make one too. However, a skilful negotiator is likely to take the concession and just wait to be offered more.

You have to learn to control the tendency to reciprocate in yourself while triggering it in the other party. The vital point is to make sure your goodwill gesture, for example, buying lunch, is entirely separate from the deal. If they feel the need to reciprocate by being generous in negotiation, so much the better for you. If not, it has only cost you lunch, you've created a bit of goodwill and your negotiating position remains intact.

■ RECIPROCITY

- ■ If someone makes a unilateral concession to you, take it and mention another area in which they could also be helpful.
- ■ If you wish to generate reciprocity, make a small gesture of generosity to the other party that is entirely unconnected to the deal. Buy the other party a drink, or lunch, or take them out to dinner.
- ■ If you feel a strong urge to reciprocate for something, just say thank you.

■ Momentum

Conversations and negotiations have a certain momentum, which you can use to your advantage. Sometimes all you need to do is to tell the other party that you are interested and they will add another sweetener in the hope of clinching the deal. If you then tell them you are more interested, sometimes they'll add more. You can play this game for quite a long time. By just keeping talking in a vaguely positive way you encourage the other party to move closer and closer to your position.

At other times in a complex deal you may find you have difficulty getting agreement on one small matter. Don't slow the whole deal down. Put that item to one side and press on with the rest of the deal on which you can reach agreement. When you have built up more agreement, when you come back to the item you set aside, the pressure to agree will be that much greater.

■ Who is running the conversation?

On the other hand, you may not want the other party to be driving the momentum of the conversation.

James is the administrator of a national museum. He was sitting through a high-energy presentation by a couple of IT salesmen about their new, sophisticated and highly expensive database and hardware package. The presentation showed their system to be the answer to any conceivable problem the museum could have. After twenty minutes, just as James was beginning to feel overwhelmed by their pitch, one of his colleagues, the finance director, interrupted.

'Excuse me,' he said, 'I'm sure you'll understand that as directors of a publicly funded institution we have a responsibility to ensure that all parties with whom we do business are both financially sound and proven to be honest. So that I can establish your status, could you possibly show me your accounts for the last financial year?'

The salesmen replied that they did not have copies of the accounts and it was not company policy to make them available for inspection at will, but—

'I see,' interrupted the finance director, and he wrote in bold clear letters at the top of his note pad, 'NO ACCOUNTS'.

As James remarked later, the presentation was continued at a rather less intense pitch from that point on. The finance director's intervention, though in itself ultimately irrelevant, reaffirmed the boundaries between his world view and theirs. A sales pitch that is designed to railroad purchasers, as this one clearly was, can be derailed by a timely affirmation of a different agenda.

If you feel that the conversation is presuming too much of you, take a moment to step back, reflect on it and identify what is wrong. Very often the first indication we do not agree with the other party's assumptions is just a feeling of unease. Pay attention to that feeling and let it guide you to what is bothering you. Then interrupt the other person's patter and point out the difference between what you think and feel and what they have presumed.

■ Politeness

It is not true that a tough negotiating stance entails a hard, tough style. It is sometimes more effective to speak very gently when you are taking a very tough position. Gentle firmness is no less powerful for being quiet. In fact, speaking quietly and softly can be immediately powerful because it forces other people to be quiet in order to hear what you have to say.

It is also useful to cultivate a habit of speaking mildly so that neither you nor the other party get caught up in emotional heat. It is easier to be in charge of your emotions if you keep a calm style. If you lose your temper or get riled it can spark off a similar response in the other party, which can lead to unnecessary antagonism. It also has an effect on you. When we make loud, emphatic or angry statements we release adrenalin into the bloodstream, which adds to our arousal, and it's twice as hard to calm down as it is to stay calm in the first place.

Being calm makes it easier to be polite, and on the whole being polite helps conversation flow more smoothly. Do not, however, feel compelled to be polite. If you have a strong position, there can be circumstances when blunt speaking is necessary and useful. Remember, they don't have to accept your offer, and they don't have to negotiate. They are still talking because they have chosen to.

A step beyond politeness is flattery. Flattery is cheap, effective and often underestimated. We all like to be told we are wonderful, that our taste is discerning, our purchases are astute and our presence compellingly attractive. Paying someone a compliment is an easy way to promote goodwill. And you make every variable that you offer work twice as hard for you if you compliment the other party on their negotiating skills. If he or she feels that their skill alone won them your concession, you flatter them. It may be that flattery is all you need to tip them into agreement.

■ Broken record

Keeping your goal in mind and being persistent are two core attributes of negotiators. Bringing them together creates a simple but powerful technique known as the 'broken record'. Just as an old vinyl record with a scratch would repeat the same phrase over and over again, a negotiator can simply keep repeating the offer. If the other party says no, they reply, 'I know that when you know more about my house/this product/the deal/whatever you will find it really is attractive. I can assure you, you are getting a bargain, so let's make a deal.' Persistence is powerful persuasion.

There is no reason for you to accept no as an answer if the other party is still in dialogue with you. You can just keep playing the broken record. Repeat your offer. If the other party says no but keeps talking to you, you can repeat your offer. You don't have to accept no until the other party has actually left the room. However, you don't want to cause the other party to break off the conversation. If you sense that immediate, direct repetition is seen as too demanding, use a more subtle variation in which you alternate between making a revised offer and repeating an earlier one.

■ Plead poverty

If you are booking a caterer for your party you could tell them you simply don't have any more money and beg them to give you a special rate because you absolutely know that their food, in particular their seafood canapés, is great. The risk is that they will agree to do the job but with reduced-cost ingredients, so mention the canapés and make clear exactly which dishes you want served. You must also decide if you are willing to book another caterer if this one turns you down on price. If not, you need to phrase your request carefully so that if you find more money you are not teaching them to squeeze you for more cash.

By the same token, if you are the caterer on the receiving end of this ploy, you should be wary of accepting it. Unless you make them trade a variable (for example, using fewer waitresses or giving you the drinks order too), you are simply training the purchaser to attack your prices.

■ Cite an authority

'My wife/husband would kill me if I let it go for that' is a powerful gambit. If your spouse is not present, your purchaser cannot argue with her or him, which allows you to present yourself as willing to trade but prevented from dropping your price by forces beyond your control. Of course, there are ways for the other party to undermine this attempt to hide behind an authority. They could, for example, appeal to a man to show his machismo, 'Show her who is boss!' Or they could offer a woman confidentiality: 'I won't tell him, so he need never know.'

If you are booking the caterer you might tell them that you really want to use them, but your boss has given you an absolute limit on your budget. This combines the poverty gambit with an authority argument. Your claim is simply that you are not empowered to offer more money, so they either accept the contract for the sum offered or you have to go elsewhere.

This is a strong gambit, but ultimately depends on the state of the competition in the market. If you can get as good, or better, service elsewhere it is a very good move. If the caterer is one of many vying for your business they have to choose between protecting their margins and maintaining turnover. However, it is more likely to work in February than in December. If you try to hammer your caterer on price in peak Christmas party season they can turn you down in the knowledge that other work will come along, and you may have trouble finding anyone else to work for you with less notice at such a busy time.

■ Promise future work

If your information gathering has revealed that the catering company is a relatively new business, or that they often have slack periods during the year, you can propose that they do this first contract at a bargain price because if it goes well you are very likely to offer more work in the future. The promise of future work is a tantalizing temptation, but unless it is specified contractually it costs nothing and guarantees nothing. So it is cheap for you to offer.

If you are the caterer you should be wary of accepting it. First, the promise is worth nothing if it is not specific. You should ask for the future work to be written into the contract: so much work over so much time with cancellation payments if it does not happen. But there is another problem too. You don't want to set a precedent of working for a low price because it is always much harder to push your rates back up if you have started low. If you start at a satisfactory rate, you can take future engagements at that price without having to fight for it.

■ Promise exposure and referrals

Vaguer than promising more work yourself, you can suggest that a good job done for you will be seen by others who will want to purchase the same thing. So, once again booking your party, you can tell the caterer all about the rich, famous and influential people who will be there and will doubtless be so impressed that they too will book their services.

Mentioning famous people is in itself a persuasive intangible, if you are able to offer it, because the caterer can enjoy the excitement of serving celebrities and can mention to future clients that such and such a film star has eaten their food.

Vague promises of exposure cost you absolutely nothing, so they are a very cheap way to make your offer more attractive. However, it is rarely advisable to push them too hard. People often feel better about such nebulous possibilities of publicity or connections with celebrity if they discover them for themselves. Drop a hint and let them pick it up – don't push it in their faces.

■ Changing focus

If one element is unpalatable to the other party, draw their attention to other parts of the deal. If they don't like your price, rather than conceding a percentage of your profit, talk to them about all the factors that make your proposal or service unique. If you are charging more than all the other ski-instructors, tell them about all the students who learned faster with you than anyone else. If your quotation for catering for the office party is more expensive than the competition, show your prospective customer your file of testimonial letters from grateful clients. Tell them that there is no point in saving money on a party if the food is mediocre.

Purchase decisions are fundamentally emotional. Your job as a negotiator is to draw the other party's attention to as many reasons as possible for them to feel good about the deal. Repeat the benefits of your offer and notice when they give verbal or non-verbal indications of appreciation of a particular point. For example, if your dad nods when you point out that he can spend the whole afternoon watching football on the telly instead of going DIY shopping and then repainting the kitchen next weekend (if he will just let you borrow the car) keep talking about the football.

Using time

If the other party is in a hurry you can gain advantage by biding your time. Don't give them the deal for free. Considering their offers, checking details, consulting colleagues and exploring possible responses are all ways to take your time about replying if you want to. Equally, you can simply say that you don't yet feel their offer is compelling enough for you.

If he is really in a hurry, he is more likely to offer a little more if you will agree the deal now. The variable is time, and it is worth more to him than you, so you can make him pay for the privilege of a speedy agreement.

If you feel under time pressure, do not show it. And be very wary of deals that call for an instant signature in order to secure a never-to-be-repeated discount. If the other party is putting you under great pressure to sign, it means they are very keen to sell. That in turn means either that they will still be keen to sell in a week's time – and probably offer a bigger discount, or they are trying to stitch you up and rip you off. In both cases, you will be better off walking out and taking your time to think about it.

Haggle over the margin

If you are purchasing, ask for a breakdown of costs. You can use it to compare the price of different elements with other providers and attack their prices. By the same token, if you are providing a composite service, never volunteer a breakdown.

In some commercial fields negotiators attack margins directly. They will say that you are making too much profit. You should never accept such an argument. The appropriate response is to point out that all businesses need to make profits and your own remuneration is simply a reflection of the value of your output. No one is forced to pay your prices; they do so because they value your services.

Many people sensibly prefer to keep private the details of their profits, precisely because some negotiators see margins as targets to attack. However, you should not confuse privacy with embarrassment. As a negotiator you have learned to value your time, your capital and everything you do, so don't be afraid to make a profit.

■ How to haggle at a market stall

Haggling in a street market is a very specific skill. It is a limited form of negotiation as the only variables at your disposal are whether you will buy, what you will buy, from whom you will buy, how much time you have and how much you will pay. Here, as an example, is how to buy a watch at a market stall.

■ MARKET-STALL PURCHASE

- Browse a few stalls at the market until you find one on which there's a watch you like.
- Ask something about a different watch and then ask the price.
- Tell the vendor that it's way too much.
- Point to another watch that's more expensive-looking, and whatever the price tell them it's too much.
- Ask if they have a cheaper one, for example, this one – pointing to the one you want.
- Whatever their price, reply that it is far too much and ask for their best price.
- Explain you don't have time to haggle, you want the very best price.
- Tell them it is far too much and move to the next stall.
- They will call after you and offer a better price.
- Looking surprised, you return. OK, you say, I asked for your best price, but you've just shown me that it wasn't your best price, because now you are offering it to me for even less. So this is probably not your best price either. Give me your real best price.

- Whatever they say, it's too much. Act as though you are about to leave again and they will ask you to buy as it is really a very good price.
- All right, you say, and pull out some money. Offer them a sum beneath their 'best price' and show them the money.
- Pick up the watch you want in one hand and hold out the money towards them. This is all the money and all the time I can spare, you say. Do you want to sell it or keep it?
- Walk away with a very cheap watch.

Using not knowing

If your offer has been rejected and you can't think of a way to improve it, you can get the other party to help you. With your optimistic and solution-focused attitude that a deal is possible, ask them to talk you through the exact nature of the difficulties they have in agreeing to your proposal. Their answer will tell you more about their values and the criteria by which they judged your offer, and it may provide you with the information to create another variable. Another way to phrase this is to ask, 'What do you have to hear in order to agree to this deal?'

Whatever the response, you can interrogate them further and find out the core values that their goals are attempting to satisfy. Even in business, where ostensibly every one simply wants to make money, more variables can be unearthed than might at first seem to be the case.

Imagine, for example, that you supply support and maintenance of IT systems to large multinationals. The purchaser at your client companies always tries to squeeze you on price. If you want to stick firmly to your price, you can ask him what his problem is with it. You can then structure the support for your price in terms of whatever he says. He might reply that he has to keep his costs down. You can respond that in the long term his costs will stay reasonable if he doesn't squeeze you so hard that you are forced to go out of business or abandon the contract. If you no longer supply him he will have the hassle of finding another provider and putting up with inferior service while the new contractors learn about the system. It's in his interests and will keep his overall costs down if he pays you a price that keeps you keen, willing and able to do business with him.

■ Splitting the difference

A common gambit in informal negotiation is an offer to split the difference. If this offer is made to you and the appearance of equality is more important to you than the reality, it may be worth accepting. But in many cases it is not necessary to do so, and not the best deal.

Splitting the difference is equitable only on the assumption that you both started at equal distance from a value that you both find acceptable. That may not be the case. Other techniques and strategies might allow you to retain a far better position in the deal, while offering the other party something else that makes it acceptable.

If you offer to split the difference, you reveal that you are willing to drop your price by at least half the difference between your positions. That reveals what the other party will perceive as padding. Furthermore, if you are doing a series of deals with one party, it is very dangerous to split the difference because you will simply train him to start at a higher and higher price so that each 'split' costs you more.

■ Creating an impression

Some offices are deliberately intimidating. Some negotiators have chairs for their guests that are lower than their own. Their offices have large and impressive reception areas with well-groomed, good-looking staff who manage to smile at you and look superior at the same time. Their coffee tables are covered in their own PR material. They drive smart cars and dress in designer clothes.

Most of us have a tendency to be impressed by the toys that money can buy, especially if they cost rather more than we can afford. It is flattering to be given a lift in someone's Rolls-Royce and more flattering still to be offered a lift in a helicopter. It can make you feel important to be invited into the VIP area or to have dinner with famous people.

But none of it pays your rent. All the props and theatre are there to bolster their egos and to intimidate you. Remember that is what they are there for. Power, as we have seen, is the perception of power. If you remain rooted in your confidence and certain of your values, you can enjoy the props for the enjoyable theatre they are. Remember to feel complimented that the other party feels the need to spend so much to impress you, and remember that they are negotiating with you because you have something they want.

The use of theatre or props may be relatively innocuous, though it is often effective. Sometimes, however, attempts at intimidation are an early indication that the other party is not keen to be completely honest. Ask yourself whether the show is hiding something. Is the other party trying to distract you from the details of the deal? Ostentatious expenditure can be an indicator of dubious business practices. When a large American company took over an English broking business, they went through the books and couldn't find all the assets they believed they had bought, so they asked the senior executives to return their cars. Four people returned between them seventeen vehicles, including a horsebox. This was not the first and will not be the last time that a lavish lifestyle concealed a less than sound financial base.

■ Just checking

Some people challenge your price out of habit. It doesn't mean they won't pay it; they just want to check they are not overpaying. There are many occasions when you don't need to drop your price. If you are the only purveyor of the stuff – or there are no others nearby – or there is a queue of other potential buyers, then you don't need to drop. So don't.

Your purchaser just needs the reassurance that they are getting the same price as others. When you tell them that others pay the same, they are satisfied. They needed to test your price just to check that it wouldn't crumble. Hold firm and they'll pay.

Don't just complain: negotiate a remedy instead

Chapter 6
Troubleshooting

❏ Complex and personal negotiations

❏ Maintaining boundaries

❏ When negotiations break down

❏ Restarting the conversation

❏ Get a solution

Having laid out the basic pattern of one-off negotiations, it is time to admit that most of the negotiations in life are not that simple. Most of us are not conducting one-off transactions in an open market with a wide range of alternatives. Most business and almost all family and emotional negotiations are more complex. However, the same attitudes underpin success, whatever the context. In this chapter we will look at some more complicated situations and how to make the most of them.

■ Commercial constraints

In the commercial world, many negotiations happen within relatively tight limits. A salesman with targets to meet negotiates with a buyer who has a bonus to earn. Each is forced to deal with the other, or another person in a similar position, because both need to maintain the turnover of their respective enterprises.

Whereas a private individual can walk away from a sale or purchase that does not suit him, a supermarket buyer cannot fail to provide his customers with the products they want. Equally a salesman cannot refuse to sell any of his produce beneath a certain price if it would mean his factory's output is no longer generating income.

These constraints tend to apply to both parties in a commercial setting, so both find their room to manoeuvre limited, and hence a certain equality is established. Within that range the same negotiation issues arise.

Occasionally, however, one side of the negotiation becomes too powerful and the other side is forced to accept their terms or go out of business. This is the situation that prevails in the English Midlands at the time of writing. The remaining small engineering firms that supply the large multinational car builders are routinely told each year that they will be offered 5 per cent less money for producing the same product. Unless they can diversify, they will eventually go out of business. In the long term the car manufacturers risk losing out too, because if they kill off all the competition and are reliant on one supplier, the boot will be on the other foot. They will become vulnerable to being forced to pay price increases because they have no alternative supplier, though this is unlikely to happen in the short or medium term because they are able to source components globally.

It is instructive to note that whenever a business establishes a monopolistic hold on a market, they try to keep at least two companies competing to supply them precisely in order to avoid being squeezed in the same way that they squeeze others.

■ Salespeople

Salespeople spend a lot of time learning how to sell, and they know the value of honesty and authenticity. As a result, most of them end up caught in a paradox. The better they can fake authenticity, the more money they make.

Brendan, whom we met earlier, says car dealers always tell two lies. The first is the lie they tell to people from whom they are buying. With a friendly, sincere and sympathetic smile, they explain how weak the market is and what a shame it is that this particular car is in need of so much expensive work. In short, they can only offer a derisory sum. The second lie is the one they tell to the purchaser. The same car, a moment later, has become a truly magnificent car, the finest example of the marque they have ever seen.

Car dealers make all their profit on the difference between the price they buy at and the price they sell at. So the better they tell those two lies, the better their business. They, like other salesmen, only negotiate if they believe it will help them make a sale. They would much prefer you to pay their asking price. They have a fund of reasons why they can't drop their price and just as many reasons why they can't pay yours.

In order to get a good deal out of them, you need to get them in the position where they believe they have nearly made a sale. Once they have scented a deal and a profit, they are reluctant to let it slip away. At this point, having made it clear how much you like the car, you can produce a long list of its drawbacks and hence why you can only pay X.

If you are buying a new car, or one so new that there is little fault you can find, visit several dealers. Get some prices from the internet and take them with you when you go to the dealers. Get each dealer to offer you his best price and then go back to the one who offered you the best. Ask him to improve on his best price, then call the second-best-price dealer and play them off against each other.

■ Good boundaries

In a business context the profit motive helps to focus everyone's attention and keep negotiations on track. In families and social situations there is no equivalent, universally respected goal. Even though everyone desires happiness and wishes to feel good about themselves, human psychology is so complex that some of the ways we do that may appear to be diametrically opposed. There is, however, one concept that helps to clarify where to begin and what can be achieved in personal negotiations. That concept is 'boundaries'.

'Boundaries' refers to the edges of our personal space and our moral and emotional responsibilities. What lies within my boundaries belongs properly to me; what lies without does not. Clear boundaries help me distinguish my emotions, my business and my affairs from those of others. Developing our boundaries is one of the most important parts of becoming an adult.

When a child is born there are no boundaries between it and its mother. She cares entirely for every aspect of the child, and the child experiences its mother as the provider of everything it needs. As children we are also open to many other people and many other patterns of interaction. As we grow up we separate and develop boundaries. We become responsible for our own welfare, and gradually a mother has to let her children make their own choices and look after themselves.

None of us manages this process perfectly, so as adults we still have the task of clarifying our boundaries. Some people expect too much of others, some too little. Some people are so caught up in their own world, or their own troubles, they have little respect for the well-being or privacy of others. If I continually interfere in your life, I am not respecting your boundaries. If you are excessively concerned about my opinions of you, you are insufficiently separate from me.

These boundary issues give rise to many of the emotional problems to which we need to negotiate solutions.

Of course, our boundaries must remain permeable to some extent, otherwise we would treat it each other as aliens, but becoming aware of our boundaries is a good way to disentangle ourselves from attitudes or expectations projected upon us by others. Good boundaries enable us to acknowledge and respect other people's agendas without feeling bound to live by them. In family life and social situations it is especially important to be able to separate your own emotional reaction from the processes of negotiation.

You can imagine your boundaries as like the white picket fence round the front lawn in old black-and-white movies of small-town America. Outside is the public space, inside is the private.

Our own gut reactions are a remarkably accurate guide to boundary violations, but as most of us have adapted to less than perfect conditions it can take a bit of detective work to find out exactly what our guts are telling us. Many of us have learned to ignore the intelligence of our emotions because of having been unable to do anything about the situation in the past.

I had a psychotherapy client once who often remarked, 'That's fine', and then changed the subject whenever she told of a painful incident from the past. She had learned to avoid noticing incidents that caused her emotional pain. By listening out for 'that's fine' she was able to notice when incidents in the present were actually violating her boundaries. If she heard herself say the words she could backtrack and pay attention to what triggered them.

When personal agendas and business mix, clear boundaries help you to keep separate issues under negotiation and personal comments. Boundaries help you separate personal or antagonistic comments from the business at hand. It is equally important to keep separate your own emotional reactions from the business of attaining the optimal goals of negotiation. The habit of noticing and respecting boundaries also helps you to keep separate the various different elements of a complex negotiation.

Finally, clear boundaries establish your own privacy. When you are negotiating arrangements with family and friends you may wish to keep some parts of your life private. When you make your boundaries you can politely and firmly establish what you are willing to discuss and to negotiate and what is your own private business.

■ Personal negotiations

In the non-commercial world, negotiations are frequently complex, ongoing and interdependent. Often negotiations have to be conducted amid an emotional atmosphere fraught with negative feelings such as fear, shame and defensiveness. These feelings render people scared and uncooperative. Hence negotiations may involve dealing with people who don't want to negotiate or people who are incompetent to do so. In other words, you are not so much doing a deal as sorting out a mess.

Lucy's neighbour, Brenda, was an unstable drug-user. Brenda would often slam doors and play music in the early hours of the morning. For years Lucy had endured the noise with the aid of earplugs and the occasional phone call to ask Brenda to keep the noise down. One night Lucy was woken at four in the morning by Brenda banging on the pipes with a hammer. When Lucy went round to remonstrate, Brenda attacked her.

The following morning Lucy told the story to the manager of the block of flats in which she lived. Frightened by the assault, Lucy felt that she could no longer complain directly to Brenda and therefore needed the management to deal with Brenda on her behalf.

The management sent a strong letter but addressed it to the wrong person, the neighbour on the other side of Lucy's flat. They subsequently failed to send any letter to Brenda, and lied to Lucy in telling her that they had done so. In the meantime Brenda had approached the management and made a complaint about Lucy.

At this point Lucy realized that she needed a strategy to deal with a situation that was unjust, far from ideal and had the potential to escalate into an undesirable feud. Brenda was not responsible enough to trust in negotiation and the management of the apartment block were not competent. Sadly, complicated and messy situations like this are all too common.

Lucy sat down with a friend and worked out a strategy. In the first place Lucy acknowledged that she felt hard done by, but realized that she had to concentrate on getting a resolution, not justice. She had enough evidence of the manager's incompetence to make his life difficult and she was keen to extract an admission from him of his errors. Her friend pointed out that that was unlikely to get him on side.

Instead she suggested that she use her evidence to hint to him that she could make his life difficult but to make it clear that she would not do so as long as he kept an eagle eye on Brenda and passed on any complaints to her forcefully and speedily.

Better still, her friend suggested that she present the whole of her proposal within the frame of 'going one down'.

Go one down

To go one down means deliberately to take a position of lower status or apparent inferiority. It is a very useful tactic in dealing with people who are aggressive, rebellious, touchy or unsure of their authority. It entails disavowing your own power or authority and appealing to the strength, intelligence or abilities of the other party. When people feel threatened or belittled they can be very resistant to any sort of cooperation or deal. By going one down you offer them the emotional position of saviour or rescuer instead of the position of adversary or victim.

When Lucy had her meeting with the manager she started by telling him how fearful she felt and how much she needed his help. She emphasized that she could not resolve the situation on her own and therefore was looking to him to uphold the regulations for everyone in the apartment building.

Lucy hinted that she felt administrative errors had been made in the past, but she emphasized that she did not feel it would be helpful to go over old ground. Looking to the future, she told him how grateful she would be for his help in ensuring that Brenda kept to the terms of her tenancy agreement in the apartment block, in particular the clauses concerning nuisance to neighbours. By explaining the degree of her concern and her determination to get the matter resolved, Lucy implied to the manager that his life would be easier if he did put pressure on Brenda, because if he did not, Lucy would continue to pester him.

Lucy's negotiations used all the characteristics of a negotiator that we looked at earlier. Lucy was persistent, goal-orientated and solution-focused. Her friend encouraged her to keep her emotional agenda separate from her desired outcome. By going one down, Lucy was able to offer the manager the role of defending her from attacks and injustice. That role was emotionally rewarding for him and helpful for Lucy.

The outcome was not perfect. Lucy realized that she would not be able to rely on the manager to do his job properly unless she kept a steady pressure on him, so she made a point of filing a nuisance report for every single time

Brenda contravened the regulations. Brenda remained a difficult and unreliable neighbour. However, Lucy's firmness and persistence kept Brenda in check and ensured that the management acted to protect her own interests.

■ Families

Imagine you want to go on holiday. Perhaps that's not very difficult to imagine. Now imagine your spouse wants to go somewhere cool and cultural and you want to lie on a beach in the sun for two weeks. Your children want to go on an adventure holiday. And, on top of that, suppose that your in-laws want to come too. This is a situation calling for negotiation.

Family negotiations are typically complex because you are trying to achieve multiple outcomes. You want an enjoyable, relaxing and refreshing holiday. So does your spouse. You both want your children to have fun, but not at the cost of giving you a nervous breakdown. It's desirable to keep your in-laws happy, but you may not relish the idea of two weeks in their company. How do you achieve as many of these goals as possible?

Once again the answer comes from applying all the characteristics outlined in Chapter 2. You may have to carry on several conversations with each of the different parties in order to find your solution.

Obviously a certain amount of research will be needed to find a holiday that can offer as much of the variety of experience required as possible. If you see a potential solution you will need to use your skills of rapport and persuasion to elicit agreement from all the different members of the family. Family dynamics are such that some people automatically reject proposals, however sensible they are, simply because someone else suggested them. These people need to be led to believe that they thought of the idea first.

Other people like to feel that they have an important influence on family decisions. They may be more amenable to accepting your idea after you have seriously suggested something less desirable first.

Every situation and every family is unique so it is impossible to design a strategy to fit all familial negotiation, but it's always the case that using the basic characteristics of the successful negotiator will enable you to negotiate efficiently, however difficult the context.

■ A gift is a gift

As we have seen, in negotiation you should never give something for nothing. By the same token, if you have made a gift to someone, it will generate resentment if you later cite it as a reason why that person owes you a favour.

A gift is a gift. Once you have given it, whatever the recipient chooses to do with it is their business. If you are still attached to it, or feel they owe you something in return, you have not completely given the gift. You will notice, however, that if you are continually generous, you train people to expect you to make gifts. If you always look after me and ask for nothing in return, why should I offer to help? I might be able to cook, clean and wash up, but if you are doing the job for me I'll just let you carry on.

In partnership and family situations it is very helpful to make clear the distinction between what is truly a gift, and times when, in fact, you will expect something in return. In reality, most of us are not quite as generous as we would like to think we are. If we admit that, and make it clear if we expect a favour to be returned, we can prevent resentment building up.

■ Complex negotiations

I have emphasized the importance of clarity, attitude, goal-setting and asking 'what if' questions to ensure you cover all possible outcomes of your negotiation. But what if you find yourself in a negotiation that is already problematic? Maybe you are taking over from someone else; maybe it's a deal that started long before you read this book. Sometimes we have to deal with situations that are less than perfect.

In a divorce, for example, there are no winners. A family is broken up and emotions can run high. If the ex-partners are too angry or hurt to talk, a third party can help negotiate the separation agreement. That person does not have to be a lawyer; they only need to be someone level-headed enough to keep the emotional agenda separate from the practical details. Even simply imagining what such a person might say can help to bring clarity to a negotiation. In dealing with strong emotions, or with difficulties such as misunderstandings or non-payment, a negotiator's attitude and skills can minimize problems and maximize progress. The points overleaf can help get negotiations going.

GETTING A DIFFICULT NEGOTIATION STARTED

- Help the other party to start negotiating – even if it involves helping them shape their proposal. In the long term you will get a better result if they buy into the process, and a solution will be found more quickly if they feel confident, optimistic and motivated. It is better that they negotiate well than that they don't negotiate at all.

- Get a dialogue going by moving up to a level at which it is possible to agree. Even something as vague as 'We would all like to resolve this problem' is a basis from which to build agreement.

- Don't admit any fault, but recognize that the other party sees the situation differently. Make sure that you distinguish for yourself between what the situation is and what you, or the other party, feel it should be.

- Acknowledge that things have not been perfect to date. As a consequence it may not be possible for all parties to get their optimum result.

- Make your initial goals modest. It is often better to find a small and relatively insignificant element on which you can build agreement. That creates a bit of trust and from there you can move on, one bit at a time, to more significant elements of the deal.

- Sometimes it can help to introduce hypothetical frames. Set aside a major disagreement and explore how something else might be resolved if the major issue was settled.

- Stay aware of your own capacity for emotional reaction. Get used to acknowledging your emotional responses and naming them. Every time you do this you make it easier to dissociate from them a little. It is when you don't monitor your emotional reactions that you identify with them and they, rather than your negotiation strategy, start driving your behaviour.

When negotiations have broken down

There is no single reason why negotiations reach deadlock. Sometimes the parties cannot find a deal that is satisfactory to both sides; other times emotional disagreements have caused one party to take offence. Maybe one party feels threatened and so feels compelled to take an entrenched position to defend their interests. Just as there is no one reason for deadlock, there is no single solution, but some of the possibilities below will help to get negotiations going again.

GETTING UNSTUCK

- Take a break and review the situation. Step back. Go for a walk around the block, go for lunch or do something else for a while.
- Ask yourself: Is it actually necessary to continue? Can you find a reasonable alternative to negotiating with this person? If so, it may be best just to walk away.
- If you feel there is merit in carrying on, re-examine the process so far. Reassess the information with which you have been working. Clearly, new issues have come to light. Are there now other gaps in your information it would be helpful to fill?
- Review your rapport. The chances are if there is stalemate that a certain amount of bad feeling and misunderstanding has arisen. Don't presume, however, that you understand the misunderstanding.
- Once again try to step into the other party's shoes. Imagine hearing yourself across the table and watching you make your points. What does it look like from over there?
- And now imagine that you can see the whole exchange from a third party's point of view. What does it look like if you imagine watching yourself and the other party, head to head?
- Separate the negotiation issues from the emotional issues. Write down how you feel, and next to it write how you would like to feel. On a separate piece of paper write down the issues being negotiated and the goals you aim to achieve. Keep these two agendas separate. The emotional issues are your business alone; the negotiation issues are all that you should take back to the negotiations. If, when they are resolved, you feel better, that is a bonus.
- When you reconvene, try to do so in a different space. The old space now has associations of disagreement, so a new one can help to create a new, more positive atmosphere.

- If you can't use a different space, bring something new into the old space. Bring in some flowers, a bowl of fruit or something else to soften the atmosphere. Try to move your positions, too. If the two teams were facing each other across a table, try to arrange the chairs in a circle. The changes you make need not be dramatic, but any change is better than none.

- Before you re-enter negotiations boost your own confidence and remind yourself of your goals.

- When you restart, acknowledge there have been problems. Re-establish, again in the most general terms, what you have in common. For example, it is likely that both parties would like to be able to put the whole matter behind them as soon as possible. Both would like to reach a reasonable agreement. Both feel strongly, but both would like the negotiations to bring about a satisfactory conclusion.

- Once you have established some agreement, however general, ask the other party how they see the problem, and gather as much detail as possible.

- At this stage do not comment or interrupt at all, other than to seek clarification. Try to use open questions, which invite sentences in reply, rather than closed questions, which can be answered with yes or no. So ask: 'What do you think are the most important issues here?' or 'How would you describe the current situation?' or 'How do you feel we can best move forward?'

- When the other party has identified a serious point of disagreement, it can be helpful to ask scaling questions. Scaling questions take the form: 'On a scale of 1 to 10, where 10 represents total impossibility of agreement and 1 represents complete agreement, where do you feel we are on this issue now?' Asking scaling questions about different elements of the negotiation will establish which areas are closer to agreement and which require more work.

- Ask: 'What for you would be the smallest real evidence that we are moving one number closer to agreement?' This question asks the other arty to consider what lies in the direction of agreement, but it does so very gently. It is important at this early stage of reviving negotiations to go slowly, so rather than try to resolve everything immediately, it may be safer to ask for the smallest possible step towards agreement rather than the largest. It is a lot easier for the other party to imagine a small step than a large one. Often it is necessary to go very slowly when re-starting negotiations and to break the deal down into much smaller parts.

■ If the going is heavy, bring your solution-focused thinking to the fore. Use Ben Furman's style of questioning. For example: 'If our next meeting were to have the possibility of producing some very small element of agreement, who would have to be there, and what would have to be on the agenda?'

■ Remember in negotiation neither party is 'right'; they simply have different points of view. The task is to create or discover a proposal that satisfies both you and the other party. As you do so, you must preserve your interests and the other party must preserve theirs. This time round, you need to take great care not to get drawn into personal or emotional responses.

■ In the end, none of us can win everything all the time, but patient solution-focused thinking can often rescue far more than you might think from apparently disastrous situations.

■ The last resort

The skills you learn and the experience you gain by negotiation will stand you in good stead, even when faced with an apparently hopeless situation.

In the late 1980s, when the former Soviet Union was just beginning to transform itself into a more free enterprise culture, all sorts of new businesses were started by individuals who did not have a standard business background. Some were former party officials; others appeared to have experience in less legitimate forms of trading.

Stuart, whom we met earlier, had chartered one of his tankers to a Russian company. The Russians paid some of the fee, but after the oil had been shipped they still owed Stuart's business some $330,000. Stuart sent them faxes, copies of the agreement, details of the liabilities and so forth, but the Russians didn't pay. Stuart consulted his lawyers, who looked at the contract and agreed that under international commercial and maritime law the Russians did indeed owe the money. But they weren't paying.

Stuart talked to his partner, Neil.

'Why don't you go and see them?' Neil said. 'Maybe it needs a personal touch.'

Stuart doesn't speak Russian, but by chance his lawyers had just taken on a trainee who was a native Russian speaker. So Stuart sent a fax to the Russians, told them he was coming to Moscow and requested a meeting.

'Delighted to meet you,' came the reply and a time and place were arranged. Stuart, with his Russian-speaking trainee, arrived at the designated hotel first; they were in the meeting room when the Russians arrived. In walked a large man with an ox-like neck, who was obviously a bodyguard. Then came a man with a briefcase, a man dressed in gangster chic who was clearly the boss, and two more bodyguards.

With his Russian-speaking assistant interpreting, Stuart went through the contract with them step by step, explaining the clauses that had been agreed and the consequent charges arising. He explained in precise detail why the Russians did in fact owe his company $330,000.

The Russians listened politely and replied that they did not agree, and anyway they had no money. They would not be drawn on the detail of their disagreement and they insisted that whatever the ins and outs of the agreement they had not got the money. After two hours, Stuart suggested they went to lunch.

The Russians agreed enthusiastically and the whole party went outside and stepped into a cavalcade of exotic limousines and jeeps. They sped through the streets of Moscow to what appeared to be an enormous private house. As they went in, Stuart discovered it was a lavish restaurant. The Russians ordered champagne, caviar, vodka and lobsters. They sat down to a quite magnificent lunch and as the wine flowed so did the conversation, about anything and everything – except the negotiations and the outstanding $330,000.

In a lull Stuart slipped $10 to his assistant and told him to give it to the maître d'hotel and tell him to make sure that at the end of the meal the bill was brought to him.

More champagne was ordered, more caviar consumed and Stuart sent another $10 to the maître d'hotel with the same message. Then they came to the end of the feast and, as requested, the bill was brought to Stuart.

He glanced at the bill, saw $650, pulled out seven $100 bills and told the waiter to keep the change.

'At that moment,' he said, 'if looks could kill, I would have died. As it was we went back to our negotiations. I told them that if they did not pay me, I would, reluctantly, have no choice but to tell my fellow members of the Shipowners' Association that they had not paid their bills and hence they would not be able to charter a ship again. Within half an hour, they had agreed to pay me $300,000.'

Within two days of his return to London, Stuart's company received the money. How did his visit get the money? Stuart had only one card to play, the threat to tell his fellow shipowners that the Russians reneged on their contract, and hence to make it difficult for them to charter another ship in the market as their reputation would be damaged. He could not make it impossible for them to find another ship, because there might be another shipowner willing to take the risk, perhaps by inflating his price so that even if he didn't collect the last instalment, he would still make money.

But the Russians, in trying to use theatre to intimidate him, inadvertently gave him another card to play against them. By picking up the bill in the restaurant Stuart was asserting his power in two ways. Not only was he showing that he was big enough and rich enough to pick up a huge bill for lunch without blinking, he also was showing that he was so confident of his own power that he was willing to take their gambit from them and play it himself. By not being intimidated he showed more power than they had. Stealing their power play was a very powerful gesture indeed.

▧ Defusing intimidation

Intimidation tactics go hand in hand with a 'win–lose' mentality. They are a poor basis for establishing trust, and like other oppressive tactics they are high maintenance. They also have the disadvantage that they tend to drive away people who would rather do business on the basis of building trust.

In the end, as in other fields, birds of a feather flock together. People who use intimidation and bullying tend to end up doing business with each other, and people who prefer to build trust, however gradually, tend to end up doing business with like-minded people. But any of us can come across people who like to use intimidation. People behave in negotiation just as they do in other areas of life. So people who are bullies in the rest of their life have a tendency to bully in negotiation.

Intimidation requires that you realize that you are being intimidated. Your best first response to intimidation is not to notice it. If, however, you do find that someone appears frightening or powerful, you can quickly change how you feel by using this visualization technique to alter your feelings.

HOW TO STOP BEING INTIMIDATED

- Make a picture in your mind of the person you have to negotiate with.
- Imagine them wearing a pink tutu and a red, plastic clown's nose.
- See them wearing shoes that are too big for them and a hat that is too small.
- Imagine them speaking with a high, squeaky voice like a little rodent in a cartoon.
- Add anything else you want until you make them look so ridiculous it makes you smile and laugh inside.
- Make the picture clear, vivid and bright so that you can recall it instantly whenever you want.
- Now remember that person's face from the last time you saw them, as though you were looking at a picture of them, right in front of you.
- Make the picture of them shrink away to a dot very quickly and at the same time imagine the picture of them looking ridiculous expanding from a dot right in front of you so that it replaces the picture of their face.
- Do this over and over again, very quickly, at least ten times a day for three days, so that it becomes automatic.
- Now whenever you see their face, you automatically have another pic ture in your mind of them looking so ridiculous that you laugh inside.

You can practise this technique by remembering someone of whom you were afraid as a child. Go through the whole exercise, step by step, and notice how your own feelings change.

This technique is an artificial way to change how you feel about someone. What is often forgotten, however, is that much of how we feel about someone is artificial or accidental anyway.

There is no reason why any of us should feel less valuable or less important than anyone else. We are all different and we all have different talents and different amounts of wealth, but each of us has a unique and irreplaceable life and our own individual point of view and understanding. What is more, what we have in common, our understanding, our humanity and our existence, is far richer and more important than what we have that is different.

As a competent negotiator you will always know that you personally are just as valuable as any other person, and each deal you strike will be one in which each of you takes responsibility for valuing the exchange according to your own principles.

In a business negotiation, both of you can make a profit, and if you wish to become rich you can probably do so. But whether or not you become rich, you never become more, or less, valuable than another person.

Believing someone else is more important than you is a powerful illusion, but in the end it is no more than that. Use your imagination to create a corrective illusion and you will restore your relationship to a rightful balance.

■ Renegotiation

Being an agent sometimes entails dismantling deals as well as putting them together. Henry, whom we met earlier, has another client, a celebrity. We'll call him Peter. Peter had agreed to write his autobiography with a ghostwriter. In the six months since the contract was signed with his publisher, Peter had found that he didn't get on with the ghostwriter. He had also become more famous and had been offered a great deal more money for his biography by a different publisher. So now he wanted to get out of the contract.

This could be seen as a problem. It's a problem for the publishers, who are not getting the book they had contracted; it's a problem for Peter, who is in an unwanted contract; and it's a problem for Henry, who has to sort it all out. However, if we look at the situation as a negotiation, we can see it quite differently. What is Henry trying to achieve? He wants to win freedom for

Peter to sign a better deal and acceptance from the publishers that their own deal will not work.

We start by clarifying what the goal of the negotiation is. Henry wants Peter free to sign the more lucrative contract and work with a different ghost-writer; he wants the publisher to accept the new situation.

Rather than itemize what was wrong from the original point of view, Henry needs to start from the assumption that the status quo is what it is and that a new agreement needs to be forged, one that needs to be framed in positive terms.

He wants to get his client out of the old contract at minimal cost in terms of both time and money. He needs to get the publisher to accept that Peter no longer is willing to work with them and to make sure that the compensation paid is as small as possible for Peter yet seen to be adequate or reasonable by the publisher. Now Henry is moving towards a solution rather than just away from a problem.

■ Negotiate a remedy

At the end of a long business trip, I booked a suite for a Friday night in a small, smart boutique hotel renowned for its luxury. The hotel provides CD players in the rooms, but each carries a request to keep the sound at a modest level as the fabric of the building was not built to modern soundproofing standards. At six o'clock the following morning, I discovered that the management had put a family with two very small, very active children in the suite above. For three hours the children ran back and forth, thumping the floorboards and completely preventing a long, luxurious lie-in. Not what I needed on this Saturday morning.

The problem was caused by the management putting the family on top of me, instead of putting me above them. They were, as evidenced by the instructions on the CD players, well aware of the limitations of the hotel's soundproofing. I complained to reception and they offered to deduct the cost of breakfast from my bill. I pointed out that the breakfast was delicious and I had no complaints about it; it was the interruption of my night's sleep that bothered me. I suggested that I would happily pay for my breakfast, which was flawless. It would be more appropriate if the room was free. They agreed.

The point of the story is never just complain, always negotiate a remedy. I felt much better for my free night, and indeed I have happily used the same hotel since. The management kept my long-term custom, and learned to provide their customers with the extra thoughtfulness that ensures they get the sleep they pay for.

◾ DON'T JUST COMPLAIN, GET A SOLUTION

- If you feel you have been wronged, do not simply make a complaint. Telling someone exactly what you think their faults are is unlikely to make them warm towards an agreement with you.
- Rather than dwell on what you think is wrong, negotiate a remedy.
- Propose what you feel will make you happier with the situation and let the other party know how they can make you happy.
- If the other party offers a remedy of their choice, don't immediately accept it just because it is on offer. Take a moment to reflect and decide for yourself if you feel it is appropriate.
- If their offer is not adequate, remind them of your proposal and invite them to give you that, or ask them to make another proposal of equivalent value for you to consider.
- Remember that many businesses, particularly insurance companies, have a policy of making low offers and paying slowly simply because they know that many people will take what they are offered.
- Keep going. In almost all commercial situations if you are persistent enough it will eventually be worth the other party's while to pay you to go away.

Read the small
print. Better still,
write it

Chapter 7
Closing

❏ Write it down and read it through

❏ Ensuring compliance

❏ The issue of fraud

❏ Walking away

❏ A good deal is good enough

In lengthy or complex negotiations it is important to keep track of what has been agreed. Each time the other party agrees to an element of your proposal, take the time to recap what they have said, ensure that they agree and you agree, and that you have a shared understanding of what you have agreed, and then write it down.

This not only saves time and creates a record of agreement, it also prevents the other party from attempting to renegotiate an element that has already been settled. If negotiations get bogged down at a later stage, a simple review out loud of what has been agreed already can revive the impetus towards full agreement.

When you feel ready to close the negotiation, check the list you have created of items agreed on the way through the negotiation against the list you created at the preparation stage. Make sure you have covered all your essential points. You can use the list you've created of items agreed along the way as the basis for a formal written agreement – see page 160.

■ Have they got enough?

Before you close it is also sensible to check that there is enough in the deal for the other party to make a reasonable profit. If you conclude a business deal in which the other party makes no money, they have no incentive to comply with the terms or continue to trade with you. Similarly, if it is a personal agreement and one party receives no benefit, they are more likely to renege on the agreement.

I once negotiated a royalty deal with two partners with which I was very happy. I was getting a good percentage of the retail price of the texts we were publishing. However, as I looked carefully at what we had agreed, I realized that my business partners were effectively paying all my tax, and paying me a royalty on the figures that included sales tax. They would end up with only 10 per cent of the profit although they were doing 60 per cent of the work. The only way they would make any reasonable money would be to cheat on me. As they were handling all the sales I had to rely on them to be honest, so I went back to them and pointed out the cost of what they had agreed. I renegotiated the deal so that all the taxes were paid before the net profit was equitably divided among us.

People are in business for all sorts of reasons, not necessarily just to make money. But if they don't make some money they go out of business. So in a commercial deal make sure there is something in it for the other party. As the saying goes, 'Always let a man make his profit.'

▓ What if

Remember to ask those 'what if?' questions. To get some peace and quiet I went away to a seaside retreat to finish writing up this book. The hotel I stayed in was quite unusual. They provided breakfast, but thereafter guests could simply use the kitchen as their own. There were plenty of decks and verandas to hide away and write. There was an honesty system for drinks and gifts. You could help yourself to beers or soft drinks and note what you had taken to be paid on departure. The atmosphere was fairly bohemian. There was a large meeting-house and the place was used for all sorts of alternative workshops from art to yoga.

The owners had made an agreement to sell it. The would-be purchasers had put down a deposit and moved in and helped to run the place but their financing had fallen through. They were there for more than a year and over and over again their finance deals fell apart and they could not come up with the balance of the money.

While I was staying there things came to a head. The owners asked the would-be purchasers to leave, and they retaliated by getting a court order to evict the owners. The would-be purchasers succeeded in getting the owners out of the hotel; they hired security and put chains across the drive. The atmosphere changed radically. Guests were challenged by the guards whenever they came and went.

Down in the village all the friends of the owners were incensed. They spend the day fuming and plotting and preparing legal documents to counter the court order, and the following day, armed with papers and lawyers and indignation, the owners and a large group of friends from the town walked back in to the hotel and repossessed it.

The would-be purchasers left and carried on their attempts to gain possession by legal means.

How had it all gone so wrong? The story is an almost perfect example of how not to negotiate, how not to conduct a sale and how not to remedy a grievance.

The vendors were too easy-going. Both parties started out very friendly and well intentioned but their contract did not cover what should happen if things went wrong. The purchasers were staying at the hotel rent-free, but also working part-time. There was no clear agreement about what payment the would-be purchasers should make for their lodgings, and what they would be paid for their part-time help at the hotel. Worst of all, there was no completion date stipulated on the contract of sale.

As more than a year had passed since the agreement was signed and still no money was forthcoming, the would-be purchasers felt that they were owed money for the work they were doing and the vendors increasingly felt they should put the property back on the market.

By the time court orders, security guards and lawyers were involved everyone had already lost out – except the lawyers.

Neither side had asked enough 'what if?' questions before they entered into their agreement. Whatever you are negotiating, however well you get on with the other party, make sure that you have a clear agreement of what to do if things go wrong. There is no shame or insult in drawing up a clear agreement, even if you are dealing with friends. Better to do so and remain friends, than not to do so and risk losing your deal and your friendship.

In general, if people are going to behave badly, they behave worse in proportion to the sums of money involved. Families fall out over inheritance, businesses fall out over profit share and lottery winners fall out over millions. If there is any possibility of money involved, make sure your agreement covers all possible liabilities, assets and income.

What if the money doesn't come through? What if market conditions change? What if the context changes? What if you change your mind? What if they default? What if they don't turn up to work? What if the car you buy breaks down as you drive home?

You may not be able to negotiate the terms you consider most favourable, but unless there is a compelling argument to the contrary it is better to have clear terms of agreement than no terms at all.

■ Terms and conditions

I once used a virtual office for a business start-up and after a reasonable amount of research agreed a deal for telephone answering and so forth with an efficient company at a good address. I was surprised to discover the first invoice was £50 per month more than we agreed. The suppliers explained that if I had mail sent to the address we were using I had to pay an extra fee. Sure enough, buried in the small print, was the liability to pay extra for what I thought I had already purchased.

If you are offered a 'standard agreement', read it very carefully and cross out any terms you disagree with. Standard agreements tend to favour the established interests (them) more than the newcomer (you).

The film industry, for example, is notorious for profit-share agreements that are never triggered. Artists are promised a share of the profits when the production company that makes the film goes into profit. However, strangely, when films gross millions at the box office, the production company doesn't go into profit. The millions of pounds and dollars are soaked up in a chain of companies through which the film is sold. A canny agent will ensure that the profit share applies to the business where the money ends up, which is not necessarily the company that made the film.

An agent, provided your deal with them is clear, simple and reasonable, is a great asset when dealing with large corporations. Ultimately, however, although they can help you negotiate, they cannot make your decisions for you. And don't ask a lawyer to negotiate for you.

■ Lawyers

Lawyers cost money and their primary job is to make watertight agreements. This means that they are very, very rarely the right people to use to negotiate. Almost anyone else, most probably you, is better placed to make the agreement. It is up to you to decide the deal you want. Then, *after* you have reached an agreement, bring in a lawyer if necessary to draw up a legally binding form of what has been agreed.

If lawyers are involved at any other stage, for example, in a dispute, they tend to be both costly and slow.

■ Completion costs

Whatever you are negotiating, think through the completion costs. Will any charges accrue other than the payment you make or receive with the other party? Are there taxes or licence fees to pay? Are there property taxes or employment liabilities to settle? If you are taking over any as yet unspecified liabilities, can you get insurance or an indemnity to cover them, and if so who pays for it? Are there transportation, installation or registration costs? Do any other tax liabilities arise? Who is liable for unforeseen third party costs?

The point at which you are about to settle on an agreement is the point at which to be pedantic about every little detail. Far better to spend time going into excessive detail now than find that your agreement is inadequate later.

Check, before you sign, that the world has not changed radically since you started your negotiations. Terence spent two and a half years concluding a property deal. By the time the deal was signed his valuation was seriously out of date. What he should have thought of before, and what he learned from that deal, was that every offer should have a defined time-frame. He should have raised his price in the interim to reflect the changes in the property market around him.

■ Fraud

Does the deal into which you are about to enter in any way compromise your legal or moral integrity? One of the fundamental principles that fraudsters or con merchants use is to get people to compromise themselves is some way, such as getting them to do something that is not entirely legal. Once someone has compromised their integrity, the fraudster is able to use that to manipulate and entrap them further.

Fraudsters known as 419ers, after the Nigerian law they violate, send out faxes and emails claiming to have huge sums of money that they wish to launder through a third-party bank account. Recipients are invited to take a share of these riches in return for their assistance. Inevitably, once they have agreed, they are asked to pay some relatively small facilitation fee, for example, $10,000. They will never see those dollars, nor any other, again. Of course, $10,000 is not a small sum at all. It only appears small because the promise of many millions of dollars has been dangled in front of them.

Remarkably, people all over the world still fall for these ruses. At the time of writing a butcher in Thurso, in the far north of Scotland, was opening his door to irate strangers who had been told that their funds had been processed through a bank registered at his address. The bank did not exist at all, and their money had long since disappeared.

■ Final checks

If negotiations have been long and complicated, by the time the end is in sight there is a tendency to want to finish it all and settle. This pressure obviously works for you in so far as it acts on the other party. But for yourself, it is helpful to pause for a moment. Before you finalize the agreement, try to take a moment to check that you are going to be happy with the proposed deal.

If possible, take five minutes out on your own to think quietly about the proposed agreement. Use the following ideas to double-check your deal.

■ DOUBLE-CHECK

- ■ Imagine what you will feel like a week or a month into the future if you have settled on these terms. It is easy and tempting to pay attention only to the benefits you will be getting, but look for the drawbacks too.
- ■ Imagine telling your friends, family or business partner about this deal. Will you feel good telling them? What are they likely to say?
- ■ Check your list. Have you achieved a satisfactory result on all the points you started with?
- ■ Check the context. Has anything material changed that has a bearing on the cost or value of elements of your deal?
- ■ Finally, check yourself. Ask yourself, are you happy with the deal itself, or is it just that the other party has made you feel happy by being charming and persuasive? If you were getting this deal from a stranger whom you really didn't care for, would you still be happy? If the answer is yes, it means that your good feelings come from the deal. If the answer is no, ask yourself if you are really ready to agree these terms.

▥ Walking away

There is no shame in walking away from a bad deal. In fact, if more people simply walked away from bad deals there would be a lot more happiness in the world. There would be fewer people paying ruinous interest on exorbitant loans, there would be fewer time-share developments and fewer houses with unsightly and expensive double-glazing.

If you are for any reason unhappy, don't sign, don't hand over the money and don't make the promise. Think about it, and think seriously about what it would be like to say, 'No thanks.' Look carefully at the downside – that is, any potential loss – and make sure you can afford to lose it before risking it in pursuit of the potential reward.

There are always more ways to achieve wealth, security or happiness than are on offer at any one time, so even a 'once-in-a-lifetime opportunity' might be the right opportunity to turn down. The next once-in-a-lifetime opportunity may be more satisfactory!

Salespeople spend a lot of their training learning how to make you feel as though you are compelled to buy. Your best defence against a salesperson's strategies is to recognize them for what they are, and to pay attention to the details of the deal, not the salesperson's chatter. How will you feel in a year's time about living with, or without, what they are offering?

▥ Write it down

When you've got the terms you want, write them all down. Very few deals require formal legal contracts, but in all cases it is worth drawing up a memorandum of agreement. This can be a formal document, if you feel it is appropriate, or just a simple letter. If it is a formal agreement you may wish to get a lawyer to draw it up. If it is a letter, write to the other party itemizing all the points you have agreed and send them two signed copies of the letter and ask them to sign them both also. They keep one for themselves and send one back to you. If there is any dispute in the future you will be able to refer to your signed letters to see what was agreed.

A lack of documentation is a sadly common factor in arrangements that go wrong and disputes that get out of hand. Inevitably in life, situations change and arrangements come to an end. If you have asked 'what if?' during your negotiation, your agreement will make provision for such happenings and you will be able to settle the matter on the basis of what was initially agreed. However, it is necessary to have and to keep safely a copy of the initial agreement.

■ Read it through

If someone else has written out the terms of your agreement always read it through before you sign.

If you are doing a deal where contracts are common and there are 'standard terms', read them too. If they are introducing extra conditions or clauses that you have not agreed, cross out the extra clauses, initial your amendment and request that the other party does too. This may provoke another round of negotiation, but do not be afraid to challenge standard clauses. They are nearly always heavily biased in favour of the author of the agreement. The fact that they are printed does not make them any more authoritative than if they were written by hand.

In some cases, of course, you may choose to accept terms that are not ideal because you judge the overall deal to be beneficial. However, beware of signing up for future commitments on the same terms. After all, if the first agreement is profitable for both parties it may put you in a stronger position in the future, putting you in a position to be able to negotiate better terms for your next deal.

■ Compliance

There are people who will negotiate a contract and then try to avoid sticking to it. Strictly speaking, the problem there is not one of negotiation, but a matter of whether someone is honest enough to stick to an agreement. Nonetheless, your negotiation skills can come to your aid.

I once had a contract to deliver a script for a certain sum of money. The day before the script was to be delivered I received a phone call from the principal backer of the project. He wanted me to deliver without receiving payment. 'There's got to be trust in this relationship,' he said. Alarm bells rang in my mind.

'Yes there has,' I replied, 'and I put my trust in the terms of the contract that we have signed.'

He got his script and I got my money.

All your 'what if?' questions will have provided you with a list of possible eventualities. Make sure that your contract stipulates specific means of redress if the other party fails to fulfil the agreement.

Ensure that every sale has a completion date, and that ownership and documentation only pass to a buyer when you have their money in your bank account.

Most problems arise from confusion and ambiguity. The more clear and comprehensive the terms of your agreement, the more likely it is that both parties will comply. Remember also to keep things as simple as possible. Every extra level of complexity is another opportunity for misunderstanding, mistakes and even fraud. The best way to prevent such problems is to negotiate clearly and firmly in the first place. By demonstrating your expertise at negotiation, you display the characteristics of a good negotiator, which are also those of someone competent and confident about achieving their goals. That is a deterrent to those who are considering trying to cheat, and will help to show them it will be better to stick to your agreement.

■ A good deal

Luke, before he established his interior design company, developed properties. He was interested in couple of adjacent houses that were being sold for £200,000 each, which at that time was a lot of money. He and his partners wanted to buy them both, but an offer was already in on one so they settled for only buying the other. They pushed to complete reasonably fast.

On the day they were about to complete, the vendor came to them. He said the other buyers were quibbling over price at the last minute – they wanted to knock £5,000 off. Luke had a lawyer in his team, and a very good line of credit at the bank. He offered the full £200,000 for completion that day, and by nine o'clock that night he had bought both houses. The other buyers were appalled, and they immediately offered Luke £210,000, then £220,000. But he was happy with his purchase, did up the houses and sold them on for a fine profit.

The moral is that if, like the other buyers, you have a good deal, don't be too greedy or try to be too clever. Or as Luke eloquently put it, 'Don't tear the arse out of a good deal.'

The most important
ingredient in a
good deal is you

Chapter 8
Establishing your style of success

❏ Keeping it simple

❏ A rewarding force in your life

❏ A force for good

Great negotiators come in all different shapes and sizes. Some are social workers and some are millionaires. All of them have learned to negotiate better deals by practising. You don't have to do large or complex deals to practise. You can do it in your everyday life.

Negotiation will help you to resolve everyday arguments, improve relationships and get better service. From now on, whenever you are dissatisfied, whether with your partner or with a purchase, don't just complain, negotiate.

Getting rapport and being solution-focused can change your own attitude, and that of others, to long-running disagreements. Negotiation is creative. By inviting other parties to make proposals and by responding to them, you come up with solutions between you that neither would have thought of on your own.

Exactly the same principles apply to small deals as to large ones. Each time you negotiate you will use only a few techniques, but each occasion will enhance your potential as a successful negotiator.

You are optimistic, curious, aware, solution-focused, thrifty, goal-orientated, tough, persistent, realistic, confident, sociable, relaxed, at ease with money, flexible, persuasive, powerful, authentic and a good listener. The more you negotiate, the more you develop these attributes. When a large or significant issue comes up, all this experience will help you to be calm, focused and successful.

■ Be yourself

You will naturally develop your own style as a negotiator. Even though you develop the same key attributes and use the same fundamental principles as other good negotiators, you will soon be doing so in your own unique way. It is rather like handwriting. We can all write the same words, but each of us does so with our own style. As you integrate the ideas you find useful from this book, you will do so in your own way, which suits and enhances your own capacities and interests.

After a couple of months, look back over the deals you have done and assess your own performance. How satisfied are you with what you achieved? Can you identify areas of technique or judgement that you can improve on?

Did you miss an opportunity? Were you too slow to pick up offers? Were you in a hurry? Did you talk too much or too fast?

The purpose of the review is not to feel bad, but to get the greatest profit from your own experience. Absolutely no one is successful all the time. Successful people are the ones who learn from everything they do. So use your review to identify areas to improve. Don't be limited by the past, or even by the ideas in this book. Be inventive. You will soon be creating your own deals to suit your own circumstances.

■ Trust

Some people are salespeople first and negotiators second. Some people care more about making money than anything else, and hence will do anything to make it. It is not that these people don't have passions, it's that their passion is making money. And some people lie.

How do you decide whether to deal with such people, and whether to trust them? In the first place, trust yourself. As we said earlier, intuition is usually remarkably accurate. But even if you were to be wrong, you would be better off trusting your own judgement than relying on someone else's assessment, because the more you use your judgement the more accurate it becomes. You learn from your own experience. If you rely on others you never develop your own judgement.

The final basis for assessment of someone's trustworthiness is their actions. If they prove themselves to be reliable and honest you will be more willing to trust them in the future. Until you have hard evidence of their honesty it pays to be cautious.

In the long term you should be actively looking for people you can trust. The more such people you know, the easier your life will be. That is why a 'win–win' style of negotiation is better than 'win–lose'. If your profit from a deal relies on the other party losing you will never be able to trust them, because they will be looking for a way to recoup their loss. You will have to be continually vigilant and spend time checking that they stick to the terms of your agreement. Worse still, you will have to start from scratch on each deal you do with them, as there will be no bank of goodwill to draw upon.

Win–win negotiations leave both parties happy. Win–win deals help to build you a network of trading partners and friends. Each one has different strengths and each one can bring their own network of friends and acquaintances. Networks such as these are worth far more than fancy business plans or MBAs. When you know you can rely on each other, everything, whether it is business or social organization, becomes easier.

In the long term, birds of a feather flock together. If you are trustworthy, you will accumulate a network of like-minded people. If you continually negotiate on a win–lose basis, win–win-style negotiators will stop trading with you, and you will end up doing most of your business with other people with a win–lose mentality. The choice is yours.

One caveat to bear in mind is that there is no point in trying to build trust in a cutthroat market. Certain markets are notoriously harsh and bring to mind the following riddle:

Q What is the best way to survive in shark-infested waters?
A Be a shark.

You will be very lucky if you do not occasionally do a deal that does not live up to your expectations, and you will be very lucky if you don't find that someone, somewhere, has taken advantage of you. If it happens, don't feel too bad, just remember the old saying, 'Screw me once, shame on you. Screw me twice, shame on me.' Don't let the same thing happen again, and don't let that person ever get in a position of trust or advantage over you.

■ Channels of communication

In principle, you can negotiate through any channel of communication, but whenever possible you should arrange a face-to-face meeting. You do not necessarily have to conclude your deal in that meeting, but it will give you invaluable information.

It is scarcely possible to quantify the amount of information you glean from meeting someone. At a pre-conscious level we learn an enormous amount about people from spending time with them, however short the time.

This knowledge is easily underestimated because it is not expressed verbally, but it informs our hunches and feelings, which in turn informs our decisions about how to negotiate. The feeling you get as you consider a particular strategy or idea is based on everything you have learned subconsciously when you met someone. You cannot get this sense of emotional status and character from a phone call or even a video link.

Once you have met someone, further communication by telephone or letter is easier to conduct and to understand. Equally importantly, a meeting gives you the chance to influence the other party through your presence. When you are optimistic, confident, solution-focused and persuasive, you make an important and positive impression.

Telephone conversations can be easily misunderstood or mis-remembered, so if you do agree something in such a conversation follow it up with a letter or an email confirming what you have understood.

Be very wary, however, of conducting negotiations by email. Email is so easy and quick to send that it gives the impression of a rich and easy mode of communication. However, the abrupt style of email messages can inadvertently cause offence and lead to misunderstanding. What you think of as a simple matter-of-fact comment could be read as a put-down.

Matters can be complicated by the fact that email can so easily be forwarded. Your private communications could be copied on to a third party who is asked to comment and before long there will be far too many opinions and ideas about what was intended and what to do next.

Emails and letters do have their uses, in particular if you want to get away from a salesman's patter and put an offer to him that he has to deal with instead of trying to talk you round to his point of view.

■ Working as a team

If you are working with someone else you can use the differences between your styles and characters to negotiate as a team. One of you can be forthright and assertive, and the other one more diplomatic.

As a team, you are more flexible and resilient. While one of you is talking, the other can be preparing alternative responses to the other party's proposal and thinking of more avenues that could advance your joint cause.

After the first meeting, if only one of you goes to subsequent meetings, you are able to stall agreement, should you wish, by explaining that you have to consult your colleague before any final decision.

Make sure that within your team you are both completely clear about the division of responsibilities and you always keep each other informed of the progress of negotiations.

■ Simple

The best deals are simple. Even if you tread a long and complicated path on your way to a deal, you should aim to keep your final agreement as simple and straightforward as possible. Complications are expensive to administer, difficult to keep track of and prone to error and fraud.

Simplicity, like reliability and common sense, is extremely valuable and often underrated. Simple ideas are also usually cheaper to carry out.

Great businessmen are frequently those who keep their common sense when people all around them are talking cobblers. They see the simple opportunities that are hidden behind the bumph and business plans of modern corporate bureaucracy.

■ Negotiating for others

You can use all the characteristics and skills we've looked at in this book to negotiate solutions between other people. Being flexible and solution-focused means you can sort out disputes between your children, friends or colleagues. When negotiating between two other parties your goal is to find common ground between them. An equally important goal is to find a way of talking about the situation that neither finds offensive and both can understand.

You will need to create rapport and to use your curiosity, your flexibility and your listening skills. It is also vital to remain independent of both parties. You can do that by being scrupulously clear about your own point of view and your boundaries. Do not tell either party that you know what they mean or that they must be right, just ask them to explain their own position carefully.

Even if you think you sympathize with one party more than the other, keep your thoughts to yourself. You might find at the next meeting that the other party tells you something that sheds an entirely different light on the situation and your sympathies might change. Furthermore, if one party believes you favour the other, they will not trust you and an agreement becomes less likely.

When each party has made their case, use the techniques and strategies we looked at in Chapter 6. Divide the issues into those they agree on, those they are fundamentally opposed to and those that are uncertain. Open your discussions by looking at a relatively minor part of the dispute. That will allow you to get a feel of the emotional situation before you touch on the bigger issues.

When disputes have lasted long enough to make it worthwhile bringing in a third party such as yourself, the chances are that a certain amount of bad feeling has built up. That tends to make both parties feel negative, defensive and hostile. In such a state of mind, few people are open to positive, friendly language. You will find therefore that you get better rapport at first by appearing cautious, drawing attention to the difficulties and being somewhat hesitant about the possibility of a solution.

As talks progress you can use all the same tools as you would when negotiating for yourself, but your goal is to move both parties towards each other, rather than towards your own interests.

It is vital that, when an agreement is in sight, both parties share the same understanding and commitment to the agreement so they can carry on without you. Your ultimate aim as a negotiator here is to make yourself redundant, so that the two parties resume a direct, cooperative relationship.

■ Making it happen

Whatever you are negotiating, for yourself or others, the most important ingredient in a good deal is you. Your enthusiasm is the key to making deals happen. Sometimes you can express that enthusiasm directly, other times you need to be more discreet, but the more you care about reaching your goals the more energy you put into your success.

This means that negotiation can be an immensely rewarding force in your life. Your own passions are the source of your most powerful motivation. The more you go for what you really want, the more powerful you will be as a negotiator. That creates a virtuous circle, because the more you do what you want, the more likely you are to enjoy it, and hence the more you apply yourself and the better you do it. Negotiation empowers you, and encourages you to realize your own dreams. You might start today by getting a rise from your boss and, who knows, you could end up buying his business.

■ Power of reputation

The better you negotiate, the better your outcomes whatever field you are working in. Success may be ten thousand pounds in the bank or it could be getting two members of the family to talk to each other after ten years of silence.

Wherever you exercise your negotiation skills you will have a positive influence, and after a while you will gain a reputation as a problem-solver and someone who gets things done. Soon your reputation will work for you, making it easier to reach solutions, then more opportunities will come your way and you will be able to pick and choose what suits you best.

■ Negotiation as a force for good

Negotiation will help you prosper in good times and survive in troubled times. If you use it to promote your values, to become more self-reliant and to create rewarding personal relationships with others, we can even say that being a skilled negotiator is a positive contribution to society.

Most obviously, negotiation is a better solution to conflict than violence, and wealth creation is better than theft. But beyond that, negotiation is a means of asserting your values above and beyond money. The mechanics of shareholding capitalism do not act to promote the personal and the authentic. We have to do it ourselves. Every time you accept something off the shelf, you contribute to the advance of impersonal consumerism. Every time you negotiate a better deal for yourself, you raise the significance of your individual perspective.

Developers would not build dull houses, supermarkets would not sell bland food and TV companies would not make tedious programmes if people refused to pay for such offerings. Of course, no single individual can change such well-established traditions of pandering to a compromise that caters for all and satisfies none. But the more you use your negotiation skills to get what you want, the more you do a service to us all. The market for off-the-shelf mediocrity will shrink as we all realize we can get something a little bit better by negotiating, and we will gradually change things for the better.

Negotiation is a tool for raising quality, just as much as for controlling prices. In a free-market economy, negotiation is a route to real freedom.

■ Your next deal

Lots of negotiators will tell you that they have been lucky. As we saw earlier, luck is made by your own attitude as much as it is by the fates. More than one successful man has observed, 'I have been lucky. And the harder I worked, the luckier I became.' I wish you luck with your next deal. I know that if you apply your own passions and release your innate negotiation skills, you will make that luck happen yourself.

Enthusiasm and integrity can work wonders. Don't feel you have to learn or use every single idea in this book or make up a hundred more. Any one negotiation will require only a few of the techniques in this book, just as one meal requires only two or three recipes from a cookbook.

The more you practise, the more confident, inventive and successful you will be. Keep practising and experimenting each day, just for fun, and the more goals you achieve and the more rewards you bring into your life, the more fulfilled you will be as you know that your success is the result of your own efforts.

You can use negotiation to increase your wealth, but used wisely it can do more than bring you money. Money can only reflect value, it cannot create it. True value comes from people and creativity. When you use negotiation to build relationships and realize your dreams you create real value. Use negotiation in every area of your life and you will find it is a creative and inspiring way to work with people.

Have fun and enjoy the deal!

Notes

Chapter 2

1 They tell the full story in *The Cloud Garden*, Tom Hart Dyke and Paul Winder, Bantam Books, London, 2004.

2 *The Luck Factor*, Richard Wiseman, Arrow Books, London, 2004.

3 For an introduction to de Shazer's work and solution-focused therapy see *Keys to Solution in Brief Therapy*, Steve de Shazer, Norton, New York, 1985.

4 For more details of Furman's work see *Solution Talk, Hosting Therapeutic Conversations*, Ben Furman and Tapani Ahola, Norton, London, 1992.

5 See *The Feeling of What Happens*, Antonio Damasio, Vintage, London, 2000. A good introduction to the therapeutic applications and biochemical research into the mind–body connection is provided in *The Psychobiology of Mind–Body Healing*, Ernest Rossi, Norton, New York, 1986.

Chapter 5

6 *No Single Thread* and *The Long Struggle*, J. Lewis and others, Brunner Mazel, New York, 1976 and 1983. Both are cited in *Life and How to Survive It*, Robin Skynner and John Cleese, Methuen, London, 1993.

7 For a more detailed and fascinating exploration of these common arguments see *Influence, Science and Practice*, Robert Cialdini, 3rd edition, Harper Collins, New York, 1993.

More essential guides available in the Personal Development series from BBC Books:

*Be Creative: Essential Steps
to Revitalize Your Work and Life*
Guy Claxton and Bill Lucas
ISBN: 0563 48764 X
CD ISBN: 0563 52331 X

*Find the Balance: Essential Steps
to Fulfilment in Your Work and Life*
Deborah Tom
ISBN: 0563 52138 4
CD ISBN: 0563 52341 7

*Get Up and Do It!: Essential Steps
to Achieve Your Goals*
Beechy and Josephine Colclough
ISBN: 0563 48765 8
CD ISBN: 0563 52346 8

*Starting Out: Essential Steps
to Your Dream Career*
Philippa Lamb and Nigel Cassidy
ISBN: 0563 52140 6
CD ISBN: 0563 52389 1

*The Confidence Plan: Essential Steps
to A New You*
Sarah Litvinoff
ISBN: 0563 48763 1
CD ISBN: 0563 52336 0

JANUARY 2005:
*Embracing Change: Essential Steps
to Make Your Future Today*
Tony Buzan
ISBN: 0563 48762 3

All titles are available at good bookstores and online through the BBC shop at
www.bbcshop.com